⌃ The Elizabeth Tower seen from New Palace Yard.

Big Ben and the Elizabeth Tower

OFFICIAL GUIDE

HOUSES OF PARLIAMENT

"a noble clock, indeed a king of clocks."

Sir Benjamin Hall MP *(1802-67), the First Commissioner of Works responsible for overseeing construction of the tower, clock and bells.*

Introduction

BIG BEN AND THE ELIZABETH TOWER

Rising high above the River Thames at the northern end of the Palace of Westminster, the tower many people affectionately refer to as 'Big Ben' – in fact the nickname for the largest of the bells it contains – is one of the greatest landmarks in the world; a symbol of Parliament, of London and of the United Kingdom.

In the dark days of the First and Second World Wars, Big Ben and its clock tower conveyed a message of strength, hope and freedom. Still today, Big Ben plays a pivotal role at times of commemoration, such as Remembrance Sunday, or of celebration, such as New Year.

Constructed in the 19th century, the tower and its contents represent the best of technology and design in Victorian Britain, including a clock of unprecedented accuracy which works as well today as when it was built over 150 years ago.

This book introduces the story of this remarkable tower, with its clock and bells, as well as the people whose exceptional vision, hard work and determination brought them into being.

You can find out more about Parliament and the history of timekeeping as well as the role that time plays in Parliament's work at the end of the book. Separate sections are included between chapters to provide more detail about related subjects.

There is more about both Houses of Parliament and the rest of the buildings in *The Palace of Westminster Official Guide*. Both guides are illustrated with material from Parliament's own collections of art, archives and photography. You will also find a wealth of detail online at *www.parliament.uk*, including information about Parliament's collections and how to plan your visit to Parliament.

"The Clock which is to be placed in the clock-tower of the New Houses of Parliament should be the very best which British science and skill can supply."

Viscount Canning *(1812-62), the member of the Government with responsibility for the Office of Works, which was in charge of rebuilding the Palace of Westminster, in a letter to George Airy, the Astronomer Royal, 20 June 1846.*

The tower at the northern end of the Houses of Parliament, with its clock and bells, is often called 'Big Ben'.

Big Ben is, in fact, the nickname of the Great Bell on which the hour is struck. Four smaller bells chime every quarter of an hour.

The tower is called the Elizabeth Tower. It was named in 2012 to mark Queen Elizabeth II's Diamond Jubilee. Before then, it was known simply as the clock tower.

The clock mechanism is officially called the Great Clock of the Palace of Westminster and Big Ben is officially the Great Bell of Westminster.

At the top of the tower is the Ayrton Light, which is lit when Parliament sits after dark.

⬆ *Palace of Westminster from Old Palace Yard*
Julian Barrow
Oil on canvas, 1990 [WOA 3416] © Julian Barrow

◀ *The Building of Westminster Bridge*
John Anderson
Oil on canvas, 1860 [WOA 1164]

The recently completed clock tower rises majestically above the twin towers of Speaker's House in this painting of March 1860. Below, construction of the new Westminster Bridge designed by Thomas Page is at an advanced stage. Made of cast iron, it replaced the earlier stone bridge of the mid-18th century.

🔈 *Perspective view of the old Palace of Westminster in the reign of Henry VIII,*
Henry William Brewer
Pen and ink drawing, 1884 [WOA 0082]

Today, this west-facing bird's eye view from above the river would look over Parliament Square and St James's Park. Drawn from the high vantage point of a hot air balloon, this Victorian reconstruction is partly fanciful but does capture the layout of the principal buildings of the old Palace in the 16th century.

The pointed Gothic towers of St Stephen's Chapel are shown in the centre foreground, surrounded by the Palace's other buildings. This was the royal family's main palace. It also housed law courts and the House of Lords and, later, the House of Commons. Westminster Hall is centre right in the image; its long sloping roof runs left to right from the end of St Stephen's Chapel.

Behind the Palace of Westminster, across Old Palace Yard, is Westminster Abbey, with the distinctive elliptical shape of the roof of its Henry VII chapel drawn on the same axis as St Stephen's Chapel.

The 14th century clock tower, which contained Great Tom, is on the far right at the edge of New Palace Yard, its single dial facing south.

The clock tower was inscribed *'Discite Justitiam Moniti [et non temnere divos]'*, a phrase in Latin from Virgil's *Aeneid* meant as a warning to lawyers. The full phrase means *'Learn the justice of watchfulness and don't tempt the gods'*. Henry VI entrusted its care to the Dean of St Stephen's College and an official, the Keeper of the Great Clock, was placed in charge – the post still exists today.

History

A clock tower first stood at the heart of Westminster 800 years ago, striking the hours on a great bell and keeping time first for a royal palace and later for Parliament. Today's tower is less than 200 years old. It was built at the height of Queen Victoria's reign at a time of great technological and industrial development.

MEDIEVAL CLOCK TOWERS AT WESTMINSTER

The first public clock at the Palace of Westminster was built between 1288 and 1292. It is said to have been the first in the country to have hands, though it probably had only a single hour hand. By this time, Westminster had already been home to a royal palace for at least 200 years.

Soon after Edward the Confessor came to the throne in 1042, he began work to rebuild a royal palace, monastery and abbey. He lived long enough to take up residence in the Palace, a building which later monarchs used and expanded, but died just eight days after the abbey was consecrated. William the Conqueror set up court in the Palace after the Norman conquest of England in 1066 and his son, William Rufus, added a great hall in 1099 which became known as Westminster Hall and is still standing today.

This first clock is believed to have been built on the orders of King Edward I and funded using a fine. The Chief Justice, Sir Ralph de Hengham (1235-1311), is said to have angered the king by altering the court record to reduce a fine that had been imposed on a poor man. The king ordered de Hengham to pay a fine which was used for the cost of constructing a clock tower with a bell near the Palace buildings in which the law courts were housed. The bell sounded the hours and this was meant to remind judges to dispense justice with impartiality. It became known as 'Great Tom of Westminster'.

Other bell towers also served the medieval Palace and surrounding buildings. At the corner of the cloistered yard to the right of St Stephen's Chapel was a tower with a bell which was used to call people to prayer. St Margaret's Church, next to Westminster Abbey, had its own bell tower and behind St Margaret's stands the Abbey's own separate bell tower, which is no longer there.

The word 'clock' originally comes from the Celtic and medieval Latin words meaning bell: *clagan* and *clocca*. In Middle Dutch, the word *clocke* was used to refer to the bell in a church tower and evolved to cover both the bell and clock as these began to be installed. The French word for bell, *cloche*, evolved from the same root (*cloque* in Old French), as did the English word 'cloak' which describes the garment's bell shape. The term 'o'clock' emerged at the start of the 20th century as an abbreviation of 'of the clock', referring to the time displayed on a clock dial. Horology, the science of measuring time, comes from the Greek word *hora* meaning a certain time or season and the suffix *-logy* from *logos* describing the study of a subject.

Between 1365 and 1367 a new clock tower was built for Edward III, only metres from where the Elizabeth Tower now stands. It stood opposite Westminster Hall in New Palace Yard, on what is now the grass lawn south of Bridge Street. It had a single dial, which faced the Palace of Westminster, and a single hand that marked the hours. Inside the tower a new bell was installed, weighing just over 4 tonnes. Originally named 'Edward of Westminster', possibly after Edward the Confessor, the bell came to be known, like its predecessor, as 'Great Tom' as well as 'Westminster Tom'.

The medieval Palace of Westminster was an important centre of the royal court and of government. Early Parliaments often met there and it became the monarch's principal residence until a fire in 1512. The resulting damage caused Henry VIII to move his court to York Place, later known as the Palace of Whitehall. Gradually, the offices required to govern the country, including the Treasury and the law courts, became established at the Palace of Westminster, and in 1547 the House of Commons started to meet in St Stephen's Chapel.

⌂ *St Stephen's Chapel (detail)*, G. Earp
Watercolour drawing, *c.* 1880 [WOA 2257]

King Edward III, in whose reign the chapel was completed, stands with Queen Philippa and a page in this Victorian reconstruction of the medieval building. The interior is resplendent with sumptuous painted and gilded decoration.

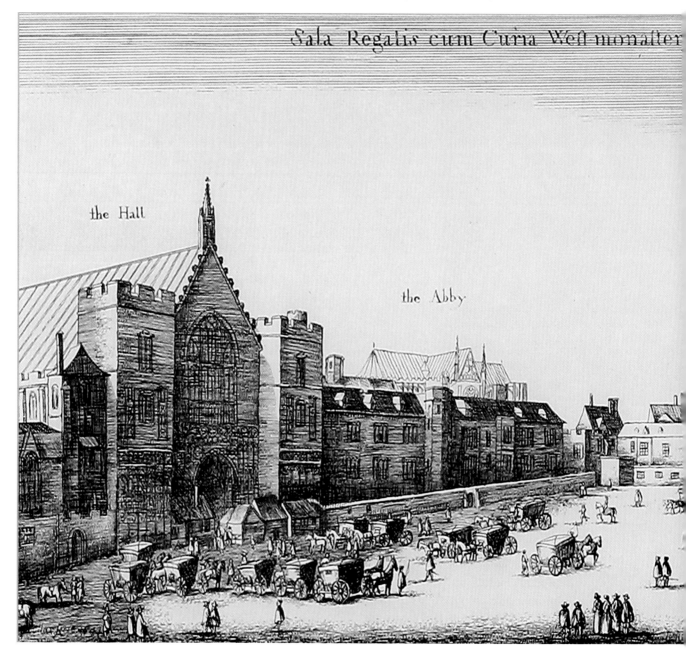

CIVIL WAR DAMAGE AND THE DEMOLITION OF THE TOWER

The clock tower in New Palace Yard stood for nearly 350 years. It was damaged during the English Civil War of 1642-49, in which forces loyal to Parliament and Oliver Cromwell fought to overthrow King Charles I. In March 1648, the King's supporters, known as Royalists, fought soldiers from Cromwell's army in New Palace Yard. The Royalists began to lose the battle and took refuge in the tower. Cromwell's soldiers laid siege to the tower. When the Royalists ran out of ammunition, they removed stones from the tower and pieces of the clock mechanism and hurled them down on to their attackers.

The damage was repaired, but the clock was said never to work quite so well afterwards. It fell into disrepair and in 1698 King William III gave it to St Margaret's Church, which stands next to Westminster Abbey. By 1707, the tower was so decrepit that it was demolished.

⤴ *Oliver Cromwell (detail)*
Hamo Thornycroft
Bronze, 1899 [WOA S29]

Since 1899 this monumental statue of Cromwell has stood in front of Westminster Hall.

↻ *Sala Regalis cum Curia West-monastery, vulgo Westminster haall*
After Wenceslaus Hollar, 17th century
Engraving, 1835
[WOA 3147A]

An early view of New Palace Yard, with Westminster Hall on the left and Westminster Abbey rising above the adjacent range of buildings. It was a busy thoroughfare, with people going to the law courts inside the Hall, and carriages lined up in the foreground outside the coffee houses by the main entrance.

On the right side of the image is the Gate House, known as the 'High Gate' or the 'King's Gate', which was the entrance from the City of London. To its right, the imposing medieval clock tower, standing approximately 100ft (30.5m) tall, dominates the surrounding buildings.

Great Tom's fate

By 1707, the original clock tower was demolished and the large hour bell, Great Tom, sold to St Paul's Cathedral for £385 17s 6d (roughly £30,000 today). The bell was dropped during its journey. It cracked but was recast in the Whitechapel foundry in 1716 and strikes the hours in St Paul's to this day. When Big Ben has been out of action for repairs, Great Tom has sometimes been used in broadcasts instead.

Turret clocks

A clock in a tower is known as a turret clock. The earliest surviving English turret clock is believed to be the one at Salisbury Cathedral which dates from around 1386. Before the mass ownership of domestic clocks and watches, turret clocks were how most people measured time even though they were not always accurate until the pendulum was invented.

Public turret clocks were constructed in buildings where people gathered or were employed, such as churches, monasteries, royal palaces, country houses – where they were usually to be found above the stable blocks – factories, and army and naval barracks.

Many early clocks had no dial and simply struck the hour on a bell, because most people, apart from the clergy and the nobility, could not tell the time.

A NEW CLOCK FOR A NEW PARLIAMENT

Following the demolition of the old clock tower in 1707, the Palace of Westminster was without one for 150 years. Apart from two sundials – one outside St Margaret's Church and one on a terraced house where the medieval clock tower stood before it was demolished – there was no way for people in the area to tell the time until a clock with a single hour hand was installed in Westminster Abbey's north-west tower in 1745.

Big Ben and the Elizabeth Tower might never have come into being if a devastating fire had not destroyed most of the Palace of Westminster on the night of 16 October 1834. The fire started after workmen burned too many unwanted tally sticks – notched pieces of wood that the Exchequer used in tax collection – overloading the furnaces beneath the House of Lords Chamber. Westminster Hall was saved but almost everything else had to be rebuilt.

The architect Charles Barry won a competition to design the new Houses of Parliament in 1835. His final plans included a clock tower. Barry initially asked his friend Benjamin Lewis Vulliamy (1780-1854), the Queen's Clockmaker, to design the clock, but after protests from other clockmakers a competition was announced to find a maker. George Airy, the Astronomer Royal, was appointed as a referee in 1846. Airy was an expert in astronomy, mechanics, optics and mathematics and knew a great deal about clocks.

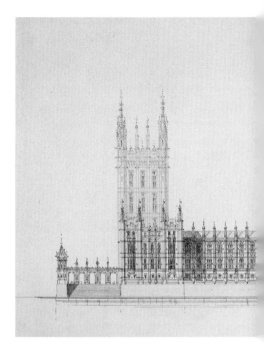

River Elevation of the New Houses of Parliament by the Office of Sir Charles Barry
Pen and ink drawing, c. 1840 [WOA 4690]

One of Barry's early designs for the waterfront elevation of the building. During the design and construction phases the scheme evolved. The clock tower is noticeably smaller than in the final design, and the roof does not yet have the two separate levels which were later introduced for the Belfry and Ayrton Light.

The Palace of Westminster on fire
Unknown artist
Oil on canvas, c. 1834 [WOA 1978]

The fire burned all night and lit up the London sky. People gathered in large numbers to witness the dramatic scene, some in boats on the water, others on the river banks.

The specifications that he devised for the clock were extremely demanding; it was to be the biggest and most accurate ever created. In 1848, Edmund Denison (1816-1905), a barrister and talented amateur horologist, became joint referee.

DEVELOPMENTS IN TIMEKEEPING

Clockmaking flourished in Britain from the second half of the 17th century, aided by Protestant craftsmen and clockmakers migrating to London to escape persecution in France when the Edict of Nantes, granting religious freedom to Protestants, was revoked in 1685. By 1700, London – in particular the district of Clerkenwell – had become an important clockmaking and watchmaking centre.

The expansion of the British Empire and international trade led to the development of the chronometer (derived from the Greek words *kronos*, meaning time, and *metron*, meaning measure), a highly accurate timekeeping device initially for use at sea. Although an unpopular tax on clocks briefly threatened the spread of timekeeping devices in 1797, it was repealed after only nine months. The term 'Act of Parliament clock' survives, however, referring to the large tavern clocks hung on the walls of inns and taverns which were said to have come about in response to the tax, though in fact they were widely used well before then.

The spread of the railway network in the 19th century required an accurate and unified system of timekeeping to prevent confusion and crashes. Previously towns and cities ran on different local times because they set their clocks using a sundial at noon, when the sun was highest in the sky, and this is later in the west of the country than in the east. Bristol time, for example, was about 10 minutes behind London time and Bristol's old Corn Exchange still has a clock with two minute hands, one showing Bristol time and the other the time in London.

By the time the competition was launched to build the Great Clock at Westminster, industrialisation and advances in technology and communications had driven huge developments in timekeeping.

The name 'Big Ben'

There are various explanations for the origin of the name. Early suggestions were to call the new bell Victoria (after Queen Victoria) or Stephen (after St Stephen, the patron saint of the chapel in the medieval Palace of Westminster). On 22 October 1856, however, *The Times* reported that *"our king of bells"* would be named *"'Big Ben' in honour of Sir Benjamin Hall".* Sir Benjamin Hall (1802–67) was First Commissioner of Works between 1855 and 1858 and oversaw the latter part of the rebuilding of the Houses of Parliament after a fire in 1834. Standing at over 6ft (1.83m), he was a tall, thin man affectionately known as 'Big Ben' and the first Great Bell is believed to have been inscribed with his name.

A less likely explanation was that the name came from Benjamin Caunt (1815-68), a celebrated heavyweight boxing champion whose nickname, 'Big Ben', was given to large objects.

⬆ *Sir Benjamin Hall, 1st Baron Llanover*
William Say after a drawing by Henry Edridge
Engraving, 1819 [WOA 2368]

Not all initial reaction to Big Ben was favourable

Sir John Pakington MP (1799-1880) wanted its *"horrible tolling"* to cease and Thomson Hankey MP (1805-93) asked, *"whether there was any chance of the bell sounding more like ordinary bells. At present it inflicted great annoyance upon the public and the House."* (*Hansard*, 15 July 1859). After the Great Bell cracked, the Earl of Derby (1799-1869) said that he *"in common with all the inhabitants of that part of London in which he lived, rejoiced"* (11 June 1860).

⌃ *A Windy Day on the Clock Tower at Westminster*
Paul Renouard
Print published by *The Graphic*, 2 February 1895
[WOA 5316]

⤳ *This is the House that Man Built....*
Unknown artist, postcard, publ. BB, London
1905-14

One of a series of postcards produced during the campaign for women's votes in the early 20th century. Parliamentary Art Collection - Reference Collection

CONSTRUCTING THE CLOCK

In keeping with 19th century innovation and progress, the Great Clock at Westminster was to push the limits of technology and become the best that British science could create. Airy required that it should be accurate to within one second every hour - something that many clockmakers believed would be impossible. It also required an extraordinary feat of engineering to cast and install what was then the largest bell in Britain.

Completing a construction of such ambition, scale and complexity depended on several exceptionally visionary and determined men and the manufacture and installation of the Great Clock and Great Bell were fraught with argument and delay (*see pages 22-3*). Eventually, however, the tower was built, and the bells installed and connected to the clock mechanism. Four huge pairs of hands began to move around the clock dials. Finally, in July 1859, almost 16 years after the tower's first stone was laid, the great hour bell, Big Ben, rang out across London for the first time.

THE CLOCK AND BELLS BECOME FAMOUS

After some initial scepticism, the clock tower became increasingly popular with the public, who began to call it 'Big Ben'. Visitors were able to get to know the tower and its remarkable contents better when it opened for Saturday afternoon tours in the late 19th century. Postcards featuring Big Ben, which were issued at the start of the 20th century by the postcard company, Valentine and Sons, and by Dent's, the company which made the clock, spread Big Ben's fame further. In 1919, it began to feature in national life as part of the service held to commemorate the end of the First World War on Armistice Day.

The BBC's first broadcast of Big Ben striking to welcome the New Year on 31 December 1923 marked the start of Big Ben's now-familiar sound entering homes across the country. Big Ben began to reach a global audience from 1932 when the BBC Empire Service, which preceded the BBC World Service, first broadcast the chimes. Remarkably, the clock kept going throughout the Second World War, and the clock tower became a focal point for British unity, resilience and determination, acquiring new stature as a symbol of democracy and freedom.

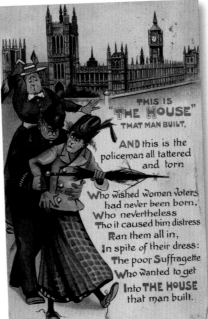

A MODERN DAY ICON

The tower is a defining icon of the United Kingdom. Its centenary was celebrated in 1959, and the year 2009 marked its 150th anniversary. In 2012, it was renamed the Elizabeth Tower to celebrate the Diamond Jubilee of Her Majesty Queen Elizabeth II. Big Ben plays an important part in marking significant national occasions and remains a steadfast feature of daily life, its deep, rolling note resounding hourly across Westminster and daily over the radio waves.

⤳ *The Clock Tower and New Palace Yard seen from the tower of St Margaret's Church Westminster*
Photographed by **Benjamin Stone MP**, July 1897
Parliamentary Archives, HC/LB/1/111/10/7

© ITV / Rex Features

At the climax of the spy thriller *The Thirty Nine Steps* (1978), the hero hangs from the minute hand to prevent the clock from reaching 11.45am and detonating a bomb.

Big Ben and popular culture

The clock, tower and bells have found their way into almost every aspect of popular culture.

One of the tower's earliest appearances was as the backdrop to a Gilbert and Sullivan operetta, *Iolanthe*, first performed in 1882. Since then, it has featured in film classics, music, works of art, posters, postcards, stamps and just about every form of merchandise imaginable from beer to bell-shaped biscuits.

The tower has been represented by countless artists from all over the world, including Claude Monet (1840-1926). The melody of the chimes can be heard in music ranging from songs such as *Big Ben is Saying Goodnight* by Alan Murray (1932) to orchestral works such as Ernst Toch's *Big Ben: Variation-Fantasy on the Westminster Chimes* (1935) and Ralph Vaughan Williams' *A London Symphony* (1912-13). On 14 November 2012, Big Ben inaugurated *2LO Calling*, a global simulcast curated by Damon Albarn that was broadcast by the BBC across all its networks to mark 90 years of BBC radio broadcasting.

Innumerable brands have realised the appeal that the image of the tower holds and pressed it into service on packaging and in advertisements since it first appeared on bottles of brown sauce in 1903. The tower and Big Ben featured in both the London 1948 and 2012 Olympic Games. Every programme and ticket for the 1948 Olympic Games included a picture of the clock tower and Houses of Parliament (*see below*).

© Mary Evans Picture Library

Coming Home to Roost
J.P. Stafford, pen and ink drawing, 1892 [WOA 6481]

A caricature about the opening of Parliament in 1892 showing key parliamentarians of the day as birds coming to roost on the clock tower. They include Gladstone (*top left*), Disraeli (*top right*), Salisbury (*bearded bird centre right*) and Harcourt (*on left of clock tower with £1 notes as a tail – he was Chancellor of the Exchequer*).

© Gary Yeowell / The Image Bank / Getty Images

⟳ Fireworks to celebrate the New Year were launched from the tower itself for the first time on New Year's Day 2012.

...ONE HUNDRED AND FIFTY YEARS LATER...

⟰ A national competition was held for young people to design a Christmas card to commemorate Big Ben's 150th anniversary. This design is by one of the finalists, Florence Roberts-Graham.

Houses of Parliament Curator's Office

Stamp Design (c) Royal Mail Group Ltd 2005

⟰⟲ The clock tower's 150th anniversary was celebrated in 2009. An exhibition and events were held. Memorabilia produced to mark the anniversary included a commemorative sheet of stamps and labels issued by the Royal Mail (above) and a lapel badge featuring a special logo (below).

Private Collection

1859-2009

The tower featured in the opening and closing ceremonies of the 2012 Olympic Games as well as in the London 2012 Festival which was held before the Games began: on 27 July, Big Ben chimed 30 times in three minutes in a mass bell-ringing event commissioned from the artist Martin Creed (*Work No.1197: All the bells in a country rung as quickly and loudly as possible for three minutes*).

Television and film classics ranging from James Bond, Harry Potter and Dr Who to the title sequence of ITV's *News at Ten* feature the tower. It has featured in children's films from classics such as Walt Disney's 1955 animated version of *Peter Pan* to more recent creations including *Harry Potter and the Philosopher's Stone* (2001). The clock tower is also integral to the plot of the James Bond movie *Thunderball* (1965), in which the clock striking seven at six o'clock would signal the Government's co-operation with a ransom demand.

The people behind the clock and the tower

The historic tower, its clock and bells came into existence because of the vision, skill and drive of a number of individuals. Each was responsible for different elements, but the whole tower could not have come about without each person pushing the boundaries of their trades and professions.

When the architect, Charles Barry, and his collaborator, Augustus Pugin, incorporated a clock tower in their designs for the Palace of Westminster, a clock and bells worthy of the new Parliament building needed to be procured to go inside it – and the Ministers and officials in charge of the Palace's rebuilding had to bring it all about. Sir Benjamin Hall MP, the First Commissioner of Works, was the man whose name came to be most associated with the tower – but others were involved too.

The Astronomer Royal, George Biddell Airy, and Edmund Beckett Denison, who together refereed the competition to decide who should build the clock, set exacting specifications and, eventually, Edward John Dent won the competition to make the clock, with his stepson, Frederick Dent, finishing and installing it after he died. The Dent family company continued to maintain the clock until the 1970s.

For 50 years, two men were employed five hours a day, three days a week to wind the clock by hand. Many people suggested labour-saving proposals. Denison said he had

The architect **Charles Barry** (1795–1860) was born on Bridge Street, across the road from where the Elizabeth Tower now stands. He designed the Travellers and Reform Clubs in Pall Mall, King Edward's School in Birmingham and the Athenaeum in Manchester. Barry is best remembered for what became his life's work, the rebuilding of the Palace of Westminster after the fire of 1834. His proposed designs in the Gothic Revival style won an architectural competition the following year, and he spent the final 25 years of his life planning and constructing the new Palace.

Barry not only conceived and controlled the entire architectural and decorative design, distilling and incorporating Pugin's vision wherever possible – including for the clock tower – but also shouldered the burden of organising the whole project, which involved answering to parliamentary committees. He was knighted in 1852 after the formal opening of the Palace. On Barry's death, a year after the famous clock and bells had begun to operate, his contribution was described as *"the greatest combination of contrivance in planning, skill in construction, business management, and true art, that the world has seen"*.

⌂ *Charles Barry*
Henry William Pickersgill
Oil on canvas, 19th century [WOA 2729]

Deryc Sands for the House of Commons media and communications service

↻ Keeping the tower and clock dials clean is a major undertaking. The tower has its own cleaner and the clock dials are cleaned by abseilers.

been asked to consider *"winding the clock by water, by a steam engine, and even by a kind of weighbridge or sinking platform to be worked involuntarily by people walking over Westminster bridge"*. The problem was solved with the installation of an electricity supply to the Palace of Westminster and, in 1913, an electric motor was fitted in the Clock Room. It winds the striking and chiming trains and is still in use today. The motor was intended to wind up the going train too, as it has three clutches, but the lighter going train is (and always has been) wound by hand. This is believed to be because the electric motor would bypass a so-called 'maintaining power' mechanism which keeps the clock going. If it were not for this mechanism, the clock would stop as the weight is being raised.

By the 1970s, Dent & Co. was finding it difficult to train and recruit clockmakers and a contract to maintain the clock was awarded to Thwaites and Reed, the company which rebuilt the Great Clock when the clock mechanism was seriously damaged in 1976.

Since 2002, the Great Clock, along with the Palace's other mechanical clocks, has been maintained by a dedicated team of skilled in-house clockmakers. Overall responsibility for maintenance lies with the Keeper of the Great Clock – the post was first established in the 14th century, though today it is combined with the role of Palace Maintenance Manager.

Augustus Welby Northmore Pugin
(1812–52) was an extraordinary creative genius and brilliant draughtsman. As a leading exponent of the Gothic Revival style of architecture, he designed some pioneering buildings, including his house at Ramsgate in Kent, and wrote several important campaigning works about architecture, notably *Contrasts* (1836) which advocated the Gothic Revival style and called for *"a return to the faith and the social structures of the Middle Ages"*.

Barry commissioned Pugin to decorate the new Palace of Westminster, including almost all of its stained-glass windows, metalwork, wood carving, wallpaper, upholstery and furniture. Indeed, Barry may have added a clock tower to his proposed design for the new Palace of Westminster at Pugin's suggestion. Pugin was heavily involved in preparing the plans, which were probably influenced by a clock tower he designed for Scarisbrick Hall in Lancashire. He confided to a friend: *"I never worked so hard in my life for Mr Barry for tomorrow I render all the designs for finishing his bell tower & it is beautiful & I am the whole machinery of the clock"*. Pugin died aged only 40, four years before the clock tower was completed.

☊ *Augustus W.N. Pugin*
John Rogers Herbert,
Oil on canvas, 1845 [WOA 2586]

↺ This Harris hawk is deployed on the parliamentary estate for pest control purposes and to discourage birds from landing on the clock dials and stonework and is named 'Denison'.

↻ The clock dials are cleaned on the outside approximately every five years – a task which involves abseiling down from the Belfry.

↺↻↻ A small team is responsible for maintenance, tours and other activities in the tower.

Three clock mechanics and a trainee mechanic maintain the clock mechanism and bells. Two are pictured with the clock mechanism and another demonstrates that a section of glass can be removed from each of the clock dials for inspections *(below)*.

Inside the Elizabeth Tower

The Elizabeth Tower is an extraordinary building in its own right and contains some of the finest 19th century craftsmanship and engineering in the United Kingdom. This chapter explores the tower's features and contents.

THE TOWER

Today, the Elizabeth Tower is a familiar sight. In 1860, however, when both it and the Victoria Tower at the other end of the Palace of Westminster were newly completed, the two towers would have loomed over the surrounding streets. London looked very different too. Work on the Thames embankment, which was designed to incorporate the new sewer and underground railway next to the river in central London, only began in 1862. Much of the river stretching from the Palace of Westminster downstream to Blackfriars and upstream to Vauxhall was a series of small wharves and muddy banks.

As the lower part of the tower was built, it must have looked as if it were going up by magic because there was no external scaffolding. Steam-powered winches were placed on scaffolding mounted on top of the walls and lifted the heavy building materials to workers standing on platforms. This method was used to move 30,000 cubic feet (850 cubic metres) of stone; 92,000 cubic feet (2,600 cubic metres) of brickwork; and many tonnes of iron girders and roofing plates.

Two separate firms of London builders constructed the tower. Grissell & Peto, who were also responsible for Nelson's Column in Trafalgar Square, built it up to the dials and John Jay's construction company built the rest.

↟ The clock tower nears completion in this detail from *The Illustrated London News* of 2 August 1856. The cast iron roof is nearly finished and the cast iron frames for the dials are being installed. [WOA 5301]

↺ The London Eye seen through the north dial. Each dial is fitted with a removable piece of glass to allow for inspections.

↻ The tower's staircase is the only way in which the top of the tower can usually be accessed. Its 334 steps wind around a narrow shaft in the south-west corner of the tower.

↻ *New Palace of Westminster*
Unknown artist, *c.* 1856
Lithograph, publ. 1858 [WOA 1656]

⬆ Charles Bradlaugh (left) in an impression of his prison suite from *The Illustrated London News* of 3 July 1880. His daughter is shown at the tea-table and his Private Secretary at a desk [WOA 6163]

↪ *Edmund Beckett Denison, Lord Grimthorpe*
Spy (pseudonym for Leslie Matthew Ward)
Colour lithographic print, published by *Vanity Fair* in 1889 [WOA 1620]

Edmund Beckett Denison (1816-1905)
Like his father, who was an MP and chairman of the Great Northern Railway who brought considerable prosperity to Doncaster, Denison was a man of drive and a fearsome adversary.

A barrister by profession and a gifted amateur clockmaker, Denison dominated the long-running controversy over the internal mechanisms for the Palace of Westminster's new clock tower. In many ways his determination was instrumental in seeing the clock and bells through to completion. Denison was a notoriously difficult colleague described as being *"one of those people who are...perfectly convinced that they know more than anybody about everything – as unhappily they often do"*.

An amateur architect, he was responsible for several buildings in Doncaster and elsewhere. However, his repairs and alterations to St Albans Cathedral were widely criticised and, after he became Lord Grimthorpe in 1886, the term *'to Grimthorpe'* came to refer to unsympathetic restoration. He was a frequent writer for *The Times*, which, in its obituary notice, called him *"ever a fighter"*.

There are 334 steps from the ground floor of the Elizabeth Tower to the Belfry, and a further 59 steps to the Ayrton Light which is housed in a lantern-like structure open to the elements. The light shines when Parliament sits at night.

Eleven floors, reached by a winding stone staircase, are situated around two central shafts. Below the clock storey, the tower originally included store rooms intended for documents. Lower down, a number of rooms were used to detain people - both Members and non-Members – whom the House of Commons resolved to commit to the custody of the Serjeant at Arms, the senior officer whose responsibilities included security. This could be done for a variety of reasons, including failure to attend the House when ordered, prevarication and appearing before a Committee in a state of intoxication. They could also have been used for people committed by the House of Lords to the custody of Black Rod. The rooms, which crossed between the tower and a wing of the main Palace, had fireplaces, pictures on the walls and dining tables. Visitors were also allowed. Today the rooms, which are private offices, can be reached only from the Palace.

Officially, the House could detain someone until the end of a session, which might have meant a number of months, although most were released after a day or two. The last time someone was detained in the tower was in 1880 when an atheist MP, Charles Bradlaugh, refused to leave the Chamber when ordered to do so during a long struggle about his swearing the oath of allegiance.

↪ Silver and ivory trowel used to lay the first stone in the clock tower. The inscription reads: *The First Stone of the Clock Tower of the New Houses of Parliament was laid by Emily, second daughter of Henry Kelsall, Esquire of Rochdale. 28th Sept 1843. Charles Barry, Architect. Thomas Grissell and Samuel Morton Peto, Builders.* Emily was Samuel Morton Peto's sister-in-law.
Parliamentary Archives, OOW/50

↪ Early design drawing of the clock tower in Charles Barry's hand. Parliamentary Archives, MOU/box7/327

Half plan at a b
showing the whole of upper part

Half plan through
Center of Clock face

Half plan at C D

c Principals to center
Gallaries

327

338

George Biddell Airy (1801-92) was a distinguished scientist who served as Astronomer Royal from 1835 to 1881. He published over 500 papers and reports, and established the Royal Observatory at Greenwich as the location of the prime meridian in 1851.

Airy worked on a wide range of scientific problems. He suffered from astigmatism and in 1825 designed the first spectacle lenses to correct the condition. In 1826, he began experiments to determine the density of the earth by swinging a pendulum at the top and bottom of Dolcoath copper mine in Cornwall to measure differences in the pull of gravity. In 1834, he was made chairman of the Commission to establish standard weights and measures. He was elected a Fellow of the Royal Society in 1836. The Airy craters on the moon and on Mars are named in his honour. His son Wilfred said that his life was: *"essentially that of a hard-working business man, and differed from that of other hard-working people only in the quality and variety of his work. It was not an exciting life, but it was full of interest".*

🎧 *G.B. Airy, LL.D., F.R.S., Astronomer Royal* Engraving from *The Illustrated London News,* 4 January 1868. Private Collection

The Clock and the Clock Room

The 5 ton (5,080kg) clock in the Elizabeth Tower is found in the Clock Room, which is reached by climbing 290 steps.

"A NOBLE CLOCK": THE MOST ACCURATE CLOCK EVER

The clock tower was a prominent feature of Charles Barry's final design for the new parliamentary buildings. Barry knew little about clocks and bells, so he asked his friend, Benjamin Vulliamy, who was the Queen's Clockmaker, to prepare plans for a clock. MPs were excited and began to call the proposed clock 'The Great Clock of Westminster'. However, to many clockmakers, including Edward Dent, the decision to award the honour of building the clock to Vulliamy without holding a competition seemed unfair. Dent specialised in chronometers, and in 1844 he built a turret clock at the Royal Exchange in the City of London which Airy described as *"the best in the world as regards accuracy of going and striking"*. Following correspondence between Airy and the parliamentary authorities, a competition was initiated in 1846 to decide who should build the new clock at Westminster, with the terms set by Airy. He drew up 15 specifications, the most demanding of which was that *"the first blow for each hour shall be accurate to a second of time."* Remarkably, the clock remains as accurate now as when it was first built more than 150 years ago. Sir Benjamin Hall MP, who was appointed First Commissioner of Works in 1855, said that it would be *"a noble clock, indeed a king of clocks."*

Such a level of accuracy had not been achieved before, and many clockmakers believed that it would be impossible in a massive turret clock with a heavy, cast-iron mechanism, not to mention four pairs of hands on such large dials. They even asked Parliament to relax the rules of the competition. Airy, however, refused to compromise and the specification remained. The time recorded by the new clock was required to be telegraphed twice a day to the Royal Observatory at Greenwich where it would be checked.

COMPETITION, ACRIMONY AND ACHIEVING THE IMPOSSIBLE

Three clockmakers were seriously interested in the contract to build the clock – Dent, Vulliamy and John Whitehurst of Derby – but Airy's demanding standards led to years of controversy, argument and delay. Ferocious rivalry broke out between the competing clockmakers – Vulliamy declared, *"Dent will never make that clock"*. The stalemate was finally broken when Denison joined Airy in refereeing the competition.

Dent finally won the competition in February 1852. He and Denison had previously worked together on a clock which was displayed at the prestigious Great Exhibition of 1851 and later installed at King's Cross railway station, where the dials can still be seen today. For the sum of £1,800 (roughly £105,000 today) Dent was to construct the new clock according to Denison's own design. Vulliamy was adamant that the design would not work and initiated legal proceedings which resulted in the contract being declared null and void at the end of 1853. Although that decision was overturned in the following year Dent did not live to see it. He died in March 1853, leaving his stepson, Frederick Dent, to complete the clock, as commemorated by the inscription on its frame:

This clock was made in the year of our Lord 1854 by Frederick Dent, of the Strand and the Royal Exchange, clockmaker to the Queen, from the designs of Edmund Beckett Denison Q.C.

INSTALLATION AT LAST

The clock mechanism was completed in 1854, but as the clock tower was still under construction, it spent five years in Dent's workshop, where it was extensively tested and improved.

The clock was finally installed in the Clock Room and officially started on 31 May 1859, to coincide with the first day of a new Parliament following the 1859 general election. It took more time to attach the clock mechanism to the bells. This was done by means of cables passing through the ceiling of the Clock Room to the Link Room above and, from there, to the Belfry. Big Ben, the hour bell, sounded for the first time on 11 July 1859, and the quarter bells in September 1859.

Edward John Dent (1790–1853) was a distinguished clockmaker who specialised in chronometers and turret clocks and established the famous Dent clockmaking company. While apprenticed in his youth to his grandfather, a candlemaker, he lodged with his cousin, Richard Rippon, a watchmaker, and found that his interest lay in horology.

Dent's talent for making accurate chronometers was soon recognised and at the age of just 24 he supplied a standard astronomical clock to the Admiralty. In 1828, he attracted the attention of the Royal Observatory which employed him to maintain and repair chronometers. In 1829 he won the prestigious First Premium Award in the seventh annual trial of chronometers, and in 1843 was awarded a prestigious contract to build the Great Clock of the Royal Exchange, London.

🎧 *Edward John Dent*
Charles Baugniet, Engraving, 1853
Reproduced by kind permission of the National Maritime Museum

🎧 John Whitehurst proposed this plan, dated 22 February 1849, for *"a separate piece of Clock Work…to be appended to the Great Clock… to break contact with a powerful magnet once every minute to regulate the other clocks in the new Palace"*. In 1846, Airy drew up 15 specifications for the new clock dealing with matters such as its *'Workmanlike Construction'* and *'accurate going'*, and requiring that *'the first blow for each hour shall be accurate to a second of time.'*

Whitehurst's plan was probably drawn up in response to a 16th specification added in 1847 which required the mechanism to *'make contact with a powerful magnet…for the purpose of producing a magneto-electric current, which will regulate other clocks in the New Palace'* – but nothing further came of this specification.
Parliamentary Archives, WHU/1/1

The clock mechanism

The clock mechanism is made of cast iron, steel and brass. It is 15ft 6in (4.7m) long and 4ft 11in (1.5m) tall and has a flatbed construction so that any one of its wheels can be removed for repair or maintenance without having to disturb the other parts.

The mechanism has three separate trains of gears. One operates the quarter bells and is known as the chiming train. Another drives Big Ben and is known as the striking train. The third is known as the going train and drives the clock hands as well as triggering the chime train every 15 minutes and the striking train every hour. Each of these three parts is driven by one of three weights.

WINDING THE CLOCK

For 150 years, the clock has been wound by hand three times a week every week of the year. As the clock is weight driven, its weights need to be wound up to the top of their weight shaft to keep the clock running. Today, this is done every Monday, Wednesday and Friday without exception. The process takes two clockmakers about an hour and 20 minutes. The clockmakers climb the tower's 334 steps to wind the weights which total about 2.5 tons (2,614kg). They are only able to wind for about ten minutes at a time because when the clock chimes or strikes, it needs the weight to drive the trains. If the clockmakers were winding, this would not work. To let the clock chime, the clockmakers stop winding and disengage the winding mechanism. After it has chimed, they re-engage

Keeping time

Airy specified that the clock's accuracy should be tested by sending a telegraphic signal twice a day to the Royal Observatory at Greenwich, where it would be checked against a highly accurate regulator clock.

A signal from the observatory was also sent to the Clock Room every hour so that clockmakers could make any necessary adjustments. The Royal Observatory's records show that the level of accuracy was well within the Astronomer Royal's requirements. He reported that *"the rate of this clock may be considered certain to much less than one second a week"*. Denison, whose ingenious designs were instrumental in achieving this remarkable standard of timekeeping said that *"anyone who has really accurate means of judging can observe that this huge cast iron machine, which has to drive through all weathers such a weight of hands as no other clock in the world, keeps better time than the best public clock you can find of common size."*

Today, the clock's time is checked against the UK's radio time signal originating from the atomic clock at the National Physical Laboratory near London.

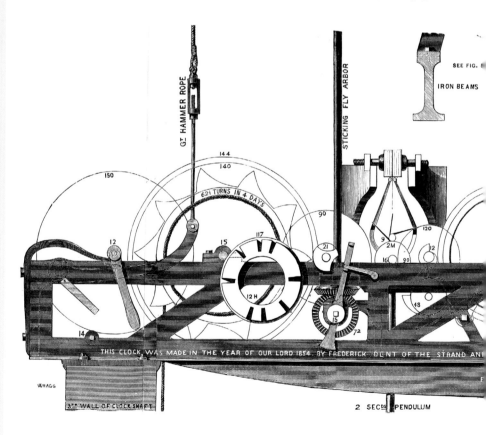

Ⓖ Edward Dent said that the clock mechanism *"should be placed in a light room...and exhibited to public view"* and, in this engraving, visitors watch the new clock being wound by hand – a task which took two men several hours a week. An electric motor was finally installed in the space beneath the clock mechanism in 1913.
Black & White, 22 November 1902.

the mechanism and start again. Today, the winding of the chime and strike weights is assisted by an electric motor, but until 1913, all three weights were wound by hand. The going train weight is still wound by hand today. After the clock has been wound, the weights gradually fall as a result of the pull of gravity and it is this action that drives each of the three trains.

KEEPING THE CLOCK TICKING

The pendulum and gravity escapement work together to keep the clock going at a constant rate. The zinc and iron pendulum is temperature compensating: its length is not affected by temperature changes because the two metals expand and contract with heat and cold in opposition to each other. The pendulum is 14ft (4.3m) long and has a heavy pendulum bob at the bottom. Altogether, it weighs 686lb (311kg) and swings from side to side every two seconds. The minute hand moves with each swing and each is marked by a loud tick as the pendulum activates the gravity escapement.

The gravity escapement gives the pendulum the impulse it needs to keep going and makes sure that each swing is regular. As the pendulum swings, it touches one of two 20 inch-long (51cm) steel gravity arms which are pivoted on either side. The weight of the gravity arm makes the pendulum swing in the other direction and the touch of the pendulum on the gravity arm unlocks the escapement, lifting the opposite gravity arm out of the way so that the pendulum can swing back and unlocking the going train so that the weight drives the minute hand forward. The pendulum swings back, touches the second gravity arm and so the process continues.

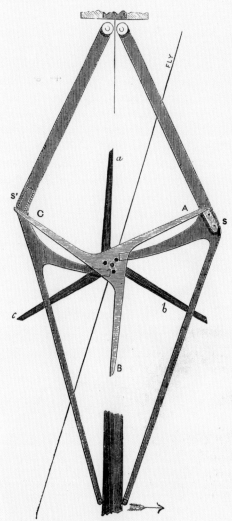

The Gravity Escapement
This sketch by Denison is of the double three-legged gravity escapement he designed for the Great Clock. In this type of mechanism, it is the pressure of the gravity arm – so named because it acts with the force of gravity – on the pendulum rod which keeps the pendulum swinging regularly. This mechanism gets its name from two three-legged wheels, labelled 'ABC' and 'abc', that turn clockwise. One stop – labelled 'S' – locks the 'ABC' teeth and the other – labelled 'S" – locks the 'abc' teeth alternately. Three pins in the centre serve to connect the two wheels and alternately lift the two gravity arms so they are ready to give the impulse to the pendulum.

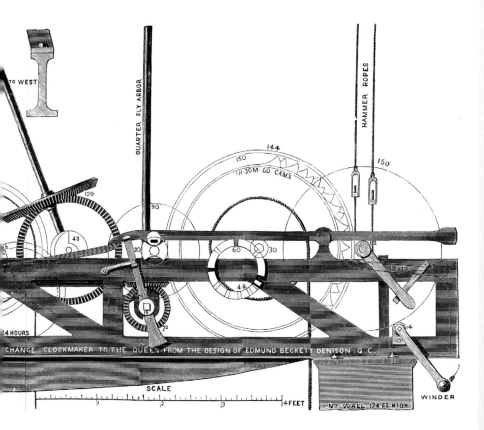

⌖ The scale diagram of 'The Great Westminster Clock' which Denison featured in his book *Clocks, Watches and Bells* published in 1903.

MAKING THE CLOCK MECHANISM

The clock mechanism was built in the Dents' London workshop. Some of the wooden patterns used to make the wheels still survive (*see below*). Once the pattern had been crafted it was put in an iron box, which was filled with sand. The sand was tamped down, the iron box opened, and the pattern was then removed, leaving an empty mould that was filled with molten iron. Once cool, the iron part was removed and further refinements were made by machine tools.

GRAVITY ESCAPEMENT MECHANISM

THIS CLOCK WAS MADE IN THE YEAR OF OUR LORD 1854 BY FREDERICK DENT OF THE STRAND AND

THE STRIKING TRAIN
makes Big Ben strike

THE GOING TRAIN
drives the clock hands and trig

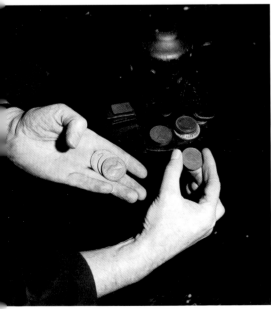

➔ THE PENDULUM

The pendulum is part of the going train. Together with the gravity escapement mechanism, it acts to keep the clock running at a constant rate.

↻ ADJUSTING THE PENDULUM

Fine adjustments are sometimes needed to keep the clock accurate. These are made with weights, including some pre-decimal pennies, which are placed on a small tray near the top of the pendulum. Adding a penny to the tray raises the pendulum's centre of gravity, making it swing infinitesimally faster and causing the clock to gain two fifths of a second in 24 hours.

THE FLY FANS

These large metal paddles are fitted to the chiming and striking trains to make the bells sound evenly. Mounted vertically and reaching the ceiling of the Clock Room, they rotate and act as governors to regulate the speed at which the chime and striking trains run. The fly fans come to a halt with a great rattle of ratchets when the mechanism stops playing. The ratchets allow the fly fans to spin on to prevent their breaking from the momentum they pick up as the bells sound.

EXCHANGE, CLOCKMAKER TO THE QUEEN, FROM THE DESIGNS OF EDMUND BECKETT DENISON C

Three subsidiary dials indicate the time – one records the hours, another minutes and the third seconds.

chiming and striking trains

THE CHIMING TRAIN
makes the quarter bells chime

THE WEIGHTS

The force of gravity acting on each of the clock's three weights provides the energy required to drive each of the three trains.

THE BARRELS
The three weights' cables are coiled onto barrels when the clock is wound. An electric motor winds the striking and chiming trains; the going train is wound by hand.

The most serious damage the clock mechanism sustained resulted from the sudden fracture of part of the chiming train in 1976. This meant that there was no check on the 1 ton (1,180kg) weight of the chiming mechanism. Wheels, gears and cams were flung at high speed around the Clock Room, and even through the ceiling. Metal fatigue was found to be the culprit, the clock having been in service for 117 years. Mild steel parts were made to replace the original cast and wrought iron ones.
Parliamentary Estates Directorate archive

A clock mechanic locks off the striking train as part of the process for stopping the clock (*see opposite*).

BREAKAGES AND STOPPAGES

Over the years, the Great Clock has suffered occasional stoppages and breakdowns.

Severe weather conditions are usually to blame. On 31 December 1961, for example, Big Ben nearly failed to ring in the New Year on time as snow had gathered on the northern dial and slowed the hands. Luckily, workmen were able to clear the snow as a section of each dial can be opened from the inside.

A flock of starlings slowed the clock by about five minutes when it landed on one of the minute hands on 12 August 1949.

There are also stories of workmen causing breakdowns. In November 1966, the clock stopped for 22 minutes because a mechanic inadvertently flicked over a ratchet on the winding mechanism.

Genuine mechanical defects are rare. The most serious breakdown occurred on the night of 5 August 1976, when the chiming train fly fan failed, dramatically destroying the chiming train (*see above*). The engineer on duty initially thought the explosion had been caused by a bomb. Fortunately, the accident happened during the night so no one was hurt.

Extensive repairs were overseen by the Palace's then Resident Engineer, John Darwin, and by the maintenance company, Thwaites and Reed. The UK National Physical Laboratory (NPL) investigated the cause of failure and tests were carried out by the Atomic Energy Research Establishment at Harwell. As a result, the NPL designed and made a safety brake. Harwell still carries out tests on the clock today. The repairs were completed in time for the bells to ring out on the occasion of the Queen's Silver Jubilee visit to Westminster Hall on 4 May 1977.

PUTTING THE CLOCK FORWARDS AND BACK

The Great Clock stops twice a year, in March and October, when the UK switches between Greenwich Mean Time and British Summer Time.

As soon as Big Ben has struck 9pm the clock mechanics silence the bell by locking off the striking train. The chimes are allowed to continue until they have sounded 9.45pm before they too are silenced.

The lights behind the clock dials are then switched off one by one in the sequence west, south, east and north, leaving the dials unlit. It is still possible to make out the hands moving swiftly towards the midnight position as the mechanics open the escapement to allow the weight on the going train to move more freely and speed up the hands. The hands take about two minutes to get to midnight – a sight which often draws spectators in the street below. When they are in position, the going train is stopped and the Great Clock is still.

The hour or two for which the clock is still provides an opportunity for inspections and repairs to be done.

When it is midnight according to the new time, the clock is restarted. The pendulum is set in motion by hand and the clock runs for two hours without any chimes or striking so that the mechanics can check its accuracy. However, it can only be properly checked once Big Ben is reinstated to strike the hour and adjustments sometimes continue until 3 or 4am.

The striking and chiming trains are unlocked just after 1.45am so that Big Ben can announce the change of time when it officially occurs at 2am. Just before 2am the dial lights are switched back on and, on the hour, the bells sound once again.

⟲ The unusual sight, which occurs twice a year, of the clock dial lights being switched off one by one until the dials are all in complete darkness before the time that they display is changed.

This clock, which is fitted above a door in the House of Commons Library, has a single mechanism for two dials – one for each side of the door.

Palace of Westminster clocks

The Great Clock in the Elizabeth Tower is one of 240 mechanical clocks still in use in the Palace of Westminster. Almost all date from the 19th century and all are still wound by hand once a week. Today's collection reflects the current and historical requirements of a working Parliament.

The oldest clock in the Palace is a highly accurate early 19th century regulator clock made by Vulliamy. It is likely to have been used to regulate the time displayed by the other clocks in the Palace.

Pugin created three designs for wall clocks when the Palace was rebuilt in the 19th century. These have oak cases and originally all had silvered brass dials. 'Sic Omnia' (an abbreviation of 'sic transit omnia' meaning 'all things pass away') or 'Tempus Fugit' ('time flies') is carved into the case below the dials. London-based clockmaker Dutton & Co. was initially asked to make 20 of them in 1851 with components supplied by different manufacturers, including John Hardman & Co. (engraved and silvered dial plates and hands), and John Webb (clock cases). Today, 92 wall clocks are still in use. The most ornate examples are in the House of Lords and the Prince's Chamber, with plainer versions in use in Committee rooms, the Libraries and offices. Pugin also designed a unique gilded brass lantern clock (*see opposite above*), though it may not have been meant for the Palace originally; it was acquired by Parliament in the 1980s. For more general office use, the Office of Works supplied circular clocks in mahogany cases. The metal dial is usually painted with Roman numerals and a monarch's initials. In many cases, the initials of later monarchs are painted on top of earlier ones: VR (Victoria Regina), EVIIR (Edward VII Rex), GVR (George V Rex), GVIR (George VI Rex) or EIIR (Elizabeth II Regina).

The silvered brass dial of this drop dial clock is engraved with the maker's name, Dutton of Fleet Street, the date, 1853, and VR for Victoria Regina.

Designed by Pugin, this is one of two bracket clocks in richly carved oak cases mounted on the walls of the Prince's Chamber in the House of Lords.

A clock installed in a desk in the gallery of the House of Commons Chamber above the Speaker's chair. The original movement has been replaced.

The Great Clock is the Palace's only external public clock, though there were apparently plans to include a further two. A clock dial was originally placed above the Peers Entrance, where today only a glazed round aperture can be seen, and the south-west turret of St Stephen's Entrance features two clock apertures, one facing west and one south – but no clock. Although clocks were planned, they were never built – a number of planned features in the Palace were left incomplete when those responsible left or died, or no funding was available.

A system of electric clocks was installed in the House of Commons in 1950 when it was rebuilt after the Second World War. A number of 'slave' dials serving the Chamber and surrounding rooms are linked to a central master clock. The clocks, including two in the Chamber, were made by Gent & Co Ltd and the architect Giles Gilbert Scott designed their cases.

A timer clock on the Clerks' table, used to time divisions, was made by F.W. Elliott Ltd. Its inscription says that the clocks in the Chamber were the gift of Northern Ireland; Commonwealth countries all contributed to rebuilding the Commons Chamber.

Today, a state-of-the-art GPS-controlled Swiss master time centre, which was installed in 2008, controls the time on nearly 200 electrical clocks in most of the Palace's public areas and both Chambers. Digital clocks display the time in both Chambers and TV screens throughout the Palace combine the function of a clock with that of an annunciator display to show what business is under way in either House.

⌂ One of many wall clocks Pugin designed for the Palace with a silvered dial and carved oak case. He also designed the wallpaper.

⌂ John Hardman & Co made this gilded brass clock to Pugin's designs. Today it is in the Prime Minister's office.

Benjamin Lewis Vulliamy (1780-1854) was the grandson of Justin Vulliamy, who moved to London from Switzerland and founded a dynasty of clockmakers. On the death of his father in 1811, Vulliamy took over the family business. He was clockmaker to the monarch and an acknowledged expert on turret clocks. He was also known for his regulator clocks – very accurate pendulum clocks – and one of these is installed in the House of Commons.

Vulliamy was originally asked to design the clock for the new Palace. His fee was 100 guineas for the plans (equivalent to about £4,500 today) plus 100 guineas if he was not chosen to make the clock. His plans were deemed inadequate by Airy, the Astronomer Royal. Vulliamy took his eventual exclusion from the project badly and publicly fell out with his successful rival, Dent. Vulliamy was a distinguished member of his profession, who served five times as master of the Clockmakers' Company and was a noted benefactor of its library and museum.

⌂ Vulliamy completed this excellent example of a regulator clock, a term given to a very accurate clock, for the Palace in 1823. It survived the fire of 1834 and is still in use today.

Time and the work of Parliament

Accurate timekeeping is crucial to Parliament's work. Members of both Houses of Parliament work to pass laws and hold the Government to account. MPs also approve taxes and public expenditure. Every day, the Palace of Westminster welcomes large numbers of members of the public on business, to visit or to watch proceedings. What is said and done in Parliament affects the lives of everyone in the country and its impact is often felt beyond the UK.

THE PARLIAMENTARY DAY
The business of the House of Commons, House of Lords and both Houses' Select Committees is subject to careful scheduling and is published beforehand. TV monitors around the building show what is going on at any moment. Both Houses' daily timetable usually follows a pattern. In the Commons, the first hour is devoted to questions to Ministers, with Prime Minister's Question Time taking place from 12 to 12.30pm on Wednesdays. Following urgent questions or statements on topical issues, the House proceeds to its main business, which may include debating legislation.

The Commons' day ends with a debate usually lasting no more than half an hour, known as an Adjournment debate, on a matter raised by an individual MP. In the Lords, there is a half-hour slot for questions at the start of each day's sitting Monday to Thursday and most of the remaining time is taken up by consideration of legislation or debates. Time is set aside on some Fridays in the House of Commons for individual MPs to debate and decide on non-Government legislation, termed Private Members' Bills.

CONTROL AND CONFLICT: THE ALLOCATION OF PARLIAMENTARY TIME
Decisions about how time is allotted are a source of conflict because the allocation of time is a way of exerting influence. Historically, there were no formal time limits. David Lloyd George's Budget statement in 1909 lasted for more than four hours, for example, and proceedings regularly continued late into the evening or through the night.

Gradually, increasing volumes of legislation and other parliamentary business made the struggle to control parliamentary time more significant and, since the 19th century, the Government has controlled most of the Commons' time. The official Opposition and smaller parties are allocated 'Opposition days' on which they select topics for discussion and, since 2010 when the Backbench Business Committee was established, MPs have also been able to bring forward motions for debate on the equivalent of around 35 days a year. MPs can also apply for two slots each week to introduce a 'ten-minute rule Bill'. These Bills rarely become law, but allow MPs to speak for up to 10 minutes in 'prime time' in the Chamber. In the House of Lords, the Government decides most of the agenda, but the subjects for some debates are chosen by ballot or in turn by the political parties and the independent Crossbench Members.

TIME LIMITS
Today, limits ensure that the Commons can get through its scheduled legislation in a timely way. A Committee considering a Bill may, for example, be instructed to finish its deliberations by a certain day, or debate on a Bill may be required to be brought to a conclusion by a certain time. Time limits may be imposed on speeches in the House if many parliamentarians want to speak in a debate. These are strictly

Traditional hourglass timers in the House of Lords Chamber.

This 19th century clock above the entrance to the House of Lords Chamber was designed by Pugin. Carved into the oak case are the words *'Omnia tempus habent'* – *'All [things] have their time'*.

enforced by the Speaker in the Commons, and sometimes done informally in the Lords. There are ornate clocks above the Speaker's Chair in the Commons and above the entrance to the Lords. In the House of Commons, debates must usually end at a particular time, such as 7pm or 10pm, and some categories of debate are limited to a set length, which may be as much as three hours or more, or as little as 45 minutes.

The use of a tactic called filibustering to take advantage of the lack of time controls led to stricter time limits for debates and speeches. MPs are said to filibuster when they make very long speeches simply to prevent the House from making a decision. Such tactics may be used, for example, in an attempt to 'talk out' a Bill. For example, on 31 July 1877, the House began a 26-hour sitting on the South Africa Bill. The use of the practice in debates on Irish legislation in the 1880s led to procedural changes.

Eight minutes is allowed for a vote if there is disagreement at the end of a debate. In this time, Members wishing to vote go into lobbies on either side of each Chamber where they are counted by 'tellers'. In the House of Commons, a clock operated by the Clerks triggers a red light two minutes after a vote is first called (the time by which tellers should be appointed), and again six minutes later, when the lobby doors are locked. In the House of Lords a similar process is followed, except that hourglasses are used to time the votes.

The Clerks, the officials of each House who are responsible for advising on practice and procedure, and for keeping the record of decisions made, operate electronic clocks to help keep track of time limits. The time at which Members start their speeches is recorded in *Hansard*, the official record of debates in Parliament, although when a succession of short speeches is given, every quarter of an hour is recorded instead, in a written echo of the Great Clock's chimes. Big Ben and the quarter chimes can be heard in both Chambers. Even in a digital age, the Great Clock and the chimes of its bells are useful reminders of the passage of time.

⬆ Timer on the Clerks' desk in the House of Commons Chamber.

↻ This clock dial is installed above the Speaker's Chair in the House of Commons Chamber. It is the largest of a set of dials of similar design which were made for the House of Commons when it was rebuilt in the 1950s and which are driven by a single master clock.

The Bells and the Belfry

Situated above the Clock Room is the Belfry, a large chamber with open sides which allow the sound of the bells to ring out. At its centre hangs the imposing mass of Big Ben, surrounded by the four quarter bells.

THE BELFRY

From the outside the Belfry is a graceful arrangement of arches below a sloping roof, but the interior shows the other side of the Victorian building project – wrought and cast iron engineered into a structure with the strength to support five bells totalling 21 tonnes in weight. Barry's original plans were for a more closed-in space, but Denison pointed out: *"The place where bells are hung on ought to be nearly all open windows… It will be a mere waste of money to get the largest bell in England to put in such a shut up place as this appears to be"*.

Inside the Belfry the massive hour bell and four quarter bells are suspended from a strong frame of wrought iron beams, braces and rivets. The frame is mounted on rollers, which sit on cast iron plates set into the walls of the tower. This design allows for movement caused by the bells' vibration and changes in temperature which might otherwise damage the structure of the tower.

THE GREAT BELL

Big Ben is a powerful presence. It weighs 13.5 tons (13,717kg) and is 7ft 6in (2.2m) high, with a diameter of 9ft (2.7m). The hammer which strikes Big Ben weighs 440lb (200kg).

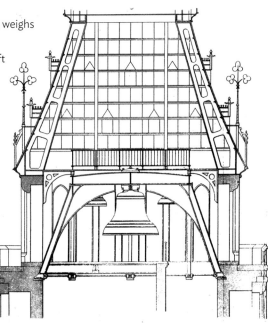

↻ Big Ben in around 1900. Gas pipes pass upwards in front of the bell to the Ayrton Light which was lit by gas until 1903. Big Ben's clapper has not yet been removed and rests on the wooden platform below the bell. The man shown leaning against Big Ben was possibly the Palace's resident engineer. Curator's Office Archive

↻ Cross-section of the Belfry showing the construction of a reinforced iron bell frame. Private Collection

CASTING AND CONFLICT

The creation of the Great Bell, like that of the clock, was a story of delay, bad communication and conflict. Charles Barry originally specified that the tower should have a 14-ton hour bell and eight quarter bells on which a melody would be rung out to mark the quarter hours. He made no further specifications and little progress was made until 1852 when Denison, whose many interests included bells and bell ringing, began to press for action. In 1855, Sir Benjamin Hall MP, the First Commissioner of Works, asked Denison to prepare a specification for the bells for the clock tower. This was fortuitous, as the clock mechanism had already been completed to a design that would link it to four quarter bells and an hour bell.

The task of casting the hour bell was a challenge. Not only was it the biggest bell to be made in Britain at that time; it also had to be made in an unconventional shape because of the design of the clock tower. The bell would have to be hoisted up the central weight shaft and a 14-ton (14,225kg) bell of normal proportions would not fit. Denison designed the bell so that it could be hoisted up on its side through the 11ft by 8ft (3.3m by 2.4m) space. He specified the mix for the bell metal as 22 parts copper to 7 parts tin.

Three bell foundries were considered for the contract to cast the bells and it was awarded to John Warner & Sons of Cripplegate in the City of London. Warner's foundry cast the quarter bells in London and the Great Bell at its Norton site near Stockton-on-Tees. When the mould was broken open, the casting was found to be intact, but the Great Bell still had to travel to London. It was taken by sea, which was commonly used for transport

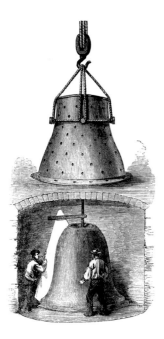

⌒ John Warner & Sons used a new patented system to cast the first Great Bell. A cast iron container (a cope) supported the mould which was made of a mixture of loam, horse hair, clay, sand and horse manure. Inside, a brick core was covered with the same mixture. The core and cope are shown being prepared for casting. *The Illustrated London News, 25 August 1856.* Private Collection

⌒ Two furnaces were specially built to cast the first bell. It took two and a half hours to melt the 18 tons (18,289kg) of metal required and five minutes to fill the mould which was in a pit. Two years later it took 20 hours to melt the metal for the replacement Big Ben and 21 minutes to fill the mould. *The Illustrated London News, 18 September 1856.* Private Collection

at the time and was the most practical way to move such a large and heavy object. Embarkation was delayed because the ship, *Wave*, was damaged when the bell was dropped as it was being loaded. However, the bell eventually arrived safely.

As the clock tower was still under construction, the bell was mounted on a temporary scaffold where it was regularly tested for 15 minutes at a time by being struck with a hammer as well as its clapper. In pursuit of an ever-louder sound, Denison insisted that an excessively large hammer be used. After 10 months of weekly testing with a 672lb (330.2kg) hammer, the bell cracked on 17 October 1857. Close inspection revealed a 4 foot-long (1.2m) crack. After fruitless wrangling over whether the blame lay with Denison for using too heavy a hammer, or John Warner & Sons for a faulty casting, the contract was put out to tender again and the cracked bell was broken up to be recast. Denison considered himself vindicated, because it was found that there was *"a great flaw in it, where the two streams of metal meeting round it had never joined. So we were in every way well rid of Big Ben the first."*

The second casting contract was given to George Mears, the master bellfounder and owner of the Whitechapel Bell Foundry and the casting was done with scrupulous care. The dimensions specified by Denison were meticulously observed, the moulds pre-heated to avoid the molten metal cooling too rapidly, and the casting left to cool gradually before the mould was broken open. The bell was tested in the same way as its predecessor – one of the only times that Big Ben has sounded with its clapper which has since been removed. Finally, it was ready to be installed in the clock tower.

The Illustrated London News noted that *"Every stage of the manufacture and erection of this magnificent bell for the Clock of the new Houses of Parliament is replete with interest."* 27 December 1856.

⌖ After it cracked, the first bell was broken up on the spot. *The Illustrated London News, 6 March 1858. Private Collection*

⌖ Big Ben arrives over Westminster Bridge. *"The Great Bell [was]...conveyed on a low truck, drawn by sixteen horses... and safely deposited in Palace-yard....The crowd collected...was so great that the police had considerable difficulty in keeping the approaches... clear."* The Illustrated London News, 5 June 1858. Private Collection

↺ Big Ben was put sideways into a wooden cage in the base of the tower and winched up to the Belfry. Lifting started at 6am on 13 October 1858 and continued until midday the following day.

The Illustrated London News, 16 October 1858 [WOA 6127]

WINCHING UP THE BELL

The system for lifting the bells was specially designed by the engineer Jabez James (1810-83) who was the son of a bell-hanger. The quarter bells were taken up through the central weight shaft by a winding crab, a form of hand-driven winch. It took six hours to raise the largest quarter bell, which weighed 4 tonnes. Work to raise the Great Bell began on 13 October 1858. The weight shaft was lined with planking and the bell was laid on its side in a wooden cradle, fitted with friction rollers. A specially forged chain, with each link individually tested, was wound on to the heavy-duty crab, which was modified so that eight men could operate it together. It took 32 hours to get the bell as far as the Clock Room. When the bell was finally hung in its place, it was tested initially by Denison using a rope attached to an internal clapper. The bell sounded pleasing, but it soon became apparent that its iron frame was not strong enough. Denison, in one of his acerbic comments on Barry's work, later noted that *"it shook under every blow of the hammers, as I had told him that it would."* Massive corner braces were added to the frame to increase its strength.

↺ This image from *The Illustrated London News* of 5 December 1857 shows the empty Belfry with a frame of iron girders from which the bells would be hung. The frame later had to be strengthened with corner braces after the bells were installed and it became clear that the original was not strong enough.

Private Collection

BIG BEN STRIKES

Big Ben first struck the hours on 11 July 1859. The quarter bells began to chime at the beginning of September 1859. At the end of that month an 11in (28cm) crack appeared in the Great Bell, which was a huge disappointment for the public who had waited so long for it to sound. The *Daily Telegraph* of 3 October 1859 announced: *"The great bell of St Stephen's tolled his last on Saturday afternoon, "Big Ben" like his predecessor, is cracked and his doleful E Natural will never again be heard booming over the metropolis."*

The new crack was the occasion for acrimonious exchanges in the press and two libel actions against Denison. For almost four years, while controversy continued, the hour was struck on the largest of the quarter bells until Airy was approached for advice on how to solve the problem. Airy thought the bell *"perfectly sound for all practical purposes"*. He suggested that the weight of the hammer be reduced and that a sturdy platform be constructed beneath the bell in case it broke up. Airy's suggestions were put into effect and Big Ben was also turned to offer a different striking surface to the hammer. Big Ben was able to resume striking the hours, although the crack altered the sound of the bell. The crack is regularly monitored. It has not grown and, although Big Ben's surface is slightly flattened in the place where the hammer strikes, the Great Bell has never been turned any further.

Jabez James (1810–1883), the son of a smith and bell-hanger, became an accomplished engineer. After coming to public attention at the Great Exhibition of 1851, at which he won a prize for his skillful scale model of the Britannia Tubular Bridge, Jabez James was contracted to produce metalwork and fittings for the Palace of Westminster. He made portions of the metalwork of the roofs and finials as well as the sturdy bellframe of the clock tower at his foundry in Lambeth. He also cast the huge iron dials and roof plates and was instrumental in the process of raising and hanging the bells in the clock tower.

Big Ben the Largest Bell Ever Cast in England. Edward Lewis & Co. This illustration is of the first Big Ben, which had to be recast, lithograph, 1857 [WOA 1414]

Bells and bell ringing

The shapes of bells have changed over time. The earliest in England are believed to have been wedge-shaped. Medieval bells were more cylindrical than modern ones. Few of these escaped being melted down when Henry VIII confiscated the property of the monasteries.

Ringing was a skilled and respected profession in medieval times, but bells only began to be rung in the characteristic English manner of today in the 17th century and are now rung in three ways. Normal ringing is accomplished when bells, each connected to a rope and wheel, are turned through 360 degrees. Chiming is heard when the bells swing through a shorter arc and are struck while moving slightly so that the clapper hits the bell more gently. Tolling is the term for a single bell being rung slowly and repeatedly, often to mark a death.

Ringing a set of bells repeatedly in order from the highest to the lowest is called ringing rounds. A variation of that order is called a change and, ringing the changes means ringing the various permutations that are possible with the given number of bells. A full peal means ringing at least 5,000 different changes without repetition.

Bells like Big Ben which are too heavy to be swung are 'hung dead' and sounded either by pulling a clapper with an attached rope or by using external hammers.

In addition to these various methods of sounding conventional bells, other arrangements may be used. The carillon, for example, is an array of many fixed bells on which tunes can be played by means of a keyboard, or clavier, connected to hammers that hit the sound bows of the bells. Carillons originated in part of the Low Countries, now in Belgium, and have existed in Britain since the late 17th century. Working examples include one with 48 notes at Bournville School in Birmingham.

THE WESTMINSTER CHIMES

The chimes of Big Ben and the quarter bells are one of the most evocative and familiar sounds in the world. Their tune was originally composed in 1793 for the church of St Mary the Great, the church of the University of Cambridge, and the musical phrase may have been taken from the accompaniment to *"I know that my Redeemer liveth"* from Handel's Messiah of 1741. They were first heard on the BBC Empire Service (the precursor to the World Service) on New Year's Eve in 1923, and the first Royal Christmas broadcast, which incorporated the chimes, was aired in 1932. The Westminster chimes later came to be associated with lines from Psalm 37:31: *"All through this hour, Lord, be my guide That by Thy Power no foot shall slide."*

⊙ Big Ben hangs from the centre of the bell frame.

⊙ An early card produced by postcard pioneers, Valentine & Sons, featuring the clock tower and music of the chimes with alternative text. This card probably dates from the early 20th century. Private Collection

⤷ The third quarter bell sounds the note of E natural.

THE QUARTER BELLS

The Elizabeth Tower's four quarter bells range in weight from 1 ton (1,016kg) to 3.9 tons (3,963kg) and sound the notes G sharp, F sharp, E and B. The fourth quarter bell, which is nearly 6ft (1.83m) tall, took on Big Ben's role of striking the hours after it cracked.

Many turret clocks before the mid-19th century did not sound the quarters and of those that did most used two bells, sounding a simple 'ting tang'.

However, from the outset, the Great Clock was intended to chime every quarter of an hour, but no decision was made at first about the number of quarter bells, or the tune they would chime. Barry had originally envisaged eight bells and Vulliamy, the clockmaker first approached by Barry, had envisaged ten.

Denison and Airy are both likely to have been behind the decision to hang four

ANATOMY OF BIG BEN

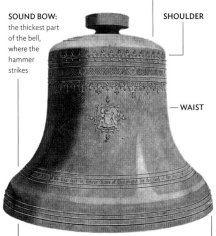

CROWN: this extends into an unusual mushroom-shaped design, and the bell is hung by means of a cast-iron collar packed with rubber, which clamps around it.

SOUND BOW: the thickest part of the bell, where the hammer strikes

SHOULDER

WAIST

THE MOUTH: the opening of the bell

THE LIP: the rim of the bell

bells to chime the quarters. Both had studied at Cambridge and would have been familiar with the four-bell chime of the Cambridge quarters – now better known as the Westminster quarters – sounded at the church of St Mary the Great in Cambridge, where Denison had been a bell ringer.

Denison's final specification for the bells required that *"the quarter bells are to be of such notes that they would be respectively the first, second, third and sixth of a peal of ten, the hour bell being the tenth"*.

The bells were cast by John Warner & Sons at their Cripplegate foundry in London. The largest was cast first, in February 1857. The other three bells were cast by mid-October, the month when the first Big Ben cracked.

STRIKING THE BELLS

The bells of the Elizabeth Tower do not swing, but are struck on the outside by hammers. One arm of the hammer curves from the top of the bell down its side, so it is within reach of the sound bow. The other arm extends horizontally from the top of the bell, and is connected to a steel cable that passes

through the Link Room to the clock mechanism in the Clock Room below.

The cable can pull the arm down so that the hammer arm opposite is raised. The bell is struck when the hammer is released.

THE LINK ROOM

This low-ceilinged room between the Belfry and the Clock Room is where the clock mechanism and the bells are connected by cables that allow the chiming and striking trains to drive mechanisms which operate the hammers to make the bells sound.

⤒ The clock mechanism and bells are connected by cables linked together in the Link Room.

Big Ben's ceremonial duties

Big Ben is used to mark some of the most solemn national occasions.

The bell tolled every 15 seconds as King Edward VII's funeral procession travelled from Buckingham Palace to Westminster Hall, where the King lay in state, in 1910. It tolled again as the procession left West-minster, and finally tolled 69 strokes, at intervals of one minute, for every year of the king's life. At King George VI's funeral on 15 February 1952, Big Ben tolled 56 strokes, one for each year of his life. As a mark of respect, the bells remained silent for the rest of the day after Sir Winston Churchill's funeral procession left Westminster Hall on 30 January 1965 and for the duration of Baroness Thatcher's funeral on 17 April 2013.

REMEMBRANCE SUNDAY

One of the most important ceremonial duties of Big Ben is the role it plays on Remembrance Sunday in November. On the eleventh hour of the eleventh day of the eleventh month in 1918, the First World War came to an end. At precisely that time the following year, the first Armistice Day commemoration took place in the United Kingdom and Commonwealth. Now known as Remembrance Sunday, that tradition has continued ever since. The royal family, politicians, faith leaders, service personnel and High Commissioners from throughout the Commonwealth gather at the Cenotaph in Whitehall to honour those who have lost their life in conflicts.

Similar ceremonies take place in towns and villages across the world, and at precisely the moment that Big Ben chimes the first stroke of the eleventh hour, a Royal Horse Artillery officer fires a single cannon shot on Horse Guards Parade, marking the start of a two-minute silence that is observed by the watching crowds in central London and broadcast to millions of people.

⬆ The gun carriage carrying Sir Winston Churchill's coffin leaves Westminster Hall for the funeral at St Paul's Cathedral, 30 January 1965.
Parliamentary Archives, HC/SA/SJ/7/3

⬆ The band of the Coldstream Guards, in their distinctive black bearskins, marches across Parliament Square in front of the Elizabeth Tower. Big Ben regularly features in national occasions.

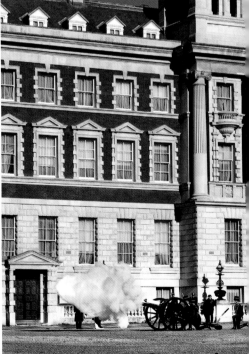

Deryc Sands for the House of Commons media and communications service

⬆➡ Signal Squadron soldiers in the Clock Room on Remembrance Sunday make sure that a cannon on Horse Guards Parade fires at exactly the moment Big Ben strikes 11.

The Ayrton Light

Acton Smee Ayrton MP after whom the Ayrton Light is named, photographed *c.1866-1869*.
Parliamentary Archives, PHO/2/2/90

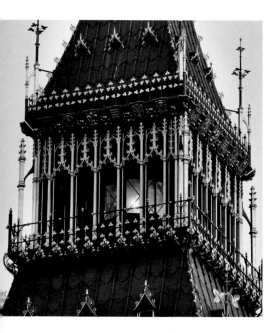

The octagonal Ayrton Light emits a powerful beam of light, which was a novelty at the time it was installed. *The Illustrated London News* 16 August 1873 reported: *"Few scenes can be conceived more singular or more beautiful...As an instance of the power of this marvellous light, it may be observed that newspapers have been read by its rays in Trafalgar-square...It is possible that all our streets a few years hence may be nightly bathed in the glorious light of electricity".*

Above the Belfry is the Ayrton Light. It is 254ft (76m) above the ground and measures 9ft (2.74m) in diameter and 12ft (3.66m) in height.

The Ayrton Light is lit when either House of Parliament continues to sit after dark. Its installation was first suggested by Acton Smee Ayrton MP (1816–86), who, as First Commissioner of Works between 1869 and 1873, oversaw the final stages of the rebuilding of the Palace of Westminster. However, several years of experimentation followed before the light that remains to this day was installed by John R. Wigham (1829-1906) of the Dublin gas engineering firm Edmundsons & Co. which supplied lights to English and Irish lighthouses.

The proposal for a light was reported in *The Times* on 7 June 1871, under the headline 'Notice to Truant MPs', but little progress was made at first. The initial idea of using lime light, which employs a gas jet to heat a cylinder of quicklime to such a high temperature that it becomes incandescent, was rejected in favour of a more powerful magneto-electric light. However, in response to a question in the House of Commons the following year, Ayrton stated that *"to erect and maintain the light would involve an expense larger, perhaps, than the circumstances would justify."* Tests to establish the best form of lighting were undertaken in April 1873. MPs made no objection to an experimental light which was installed soon afterwards. This provisional light was retained until a permanent gas-powered light was finally installed in 1885.

68 gas burners whose jets merged into a single great flame illuminated the new gas light and a workman had to mount the stairs to the top of the clock tower every evening at sunset to light the flame, although it could be extinguished by means of a valve in the Engineers' Control Room.

Early engravings show that this light shone only to the west, in the direction of Buckingham Palace – it has been suggested that Queen Victoria, who liked to keep abreast of parliamentary business, could use it to tell when she might expect Ministers to start arriving after the House had finished sitting. In 1892, Wigham suggested that lenses be used to *"spread the light round the whole of London"* and, later that year, installed a new lighthouse-style light, which was 9.5ft (2.9m) higher than the previous one and shone in all directions. It was subsequently suggested that a different coloured light could shine when a division or vote was taking place, but this was thought too costly. Since 1903, the Ayrton Light has used electric lighting.

The surrounding streets had been lit by gas lamps since the early 19th century, but even by the 1880s the level of night-time lighting was very low. Given the general absence of tall buildings in the vicinity at that time, when it first operated the Ayrton Light – like the illuminated dials of the clock itself – must have been an impressive sight.

Relighting the Ayrton Light in 1945

The Ayrton Light remained unlit throughout the Second World War. It was lit once more as war drew to a close on 24 April 1945, when the House of Commons Journal records:

"Mr Speaker addressed the House, as followeth: May I be allowed to make a slight interruption in the proceedings? In peace-time the lantern light above Big Ben always shone out after sunset in order to show that the House of Commons was at work. For five years, seven months and twenty-three days, this light has now been extinguished. When I press this switch our lantern light will shine once more. In so doing, I pray that, with God's blessing, this light will shine henceforth not only as an outward and visible sign that the Parliament of a free people is assembled in free debate, but also, that it may shine as a beacon of sure hope in a sadly torn and distracted world. I now turn on our lantern light."

🔊 The Ayrton Light was to have had a dual function: to illuminate the streets below and to indicate when the House of Commons was sitting. *The Illustrated London News*, 16 August 1873. Private Collection

Big Ben in wartime

Big Ben's place in people's affections was cemented during the First and Second World Wars. It came to embody the spirit of wartime resilience.

In the First World War, Big Ben and the quarter bells were silenced, and the clock dials darkened at night to prevent attack from German Zeppelin airships. Big Ben sounded to announce the end of the war at 11am on 11 November 1918 and has, since 1919, marked the start of two minutes' silence at 11am on every Remembrance Sunday.

In the Second World War, the bells continued to ring and be broadcast as the sound was thought to be reassuring and good for public morale. The enemy aircraft flew at higher altitudes than the First World War Zeppelins so it was not felt necessary to silence the bells. The clock dials and Ayrton Light were not lit, however, as it was feared that the light would serve to guide enemy pilots.

For three months from June 1944, a recording of the bells was broadcast. It was thought that hearing bombs fall in the background, or worse, might be bad for morale and that the enemy might be able to pick up information from the background sounds in live trans- missions. The public could tell that they were recordings and rumours spread that the clock tower had been damaged. Live transmission was quickly restored.

⬆ The gutted remains of the House of Commons Chamber in the aftermath of bombing in the Second World War. The south side of the clock tower was also damaged.
Parliamentary Estates Directorate Archive

Throughout both wars, the Great Clock kept near-perfect time and was not stopped on a single occasion as a result of enemy action. The clock tower was damaged by bombs which destroyed the Commons Chamber on the night of 10–11 May 1941. The glass in the south dial was broken, but the clock mechanism and bells continued to function as usual.

↻ *The Palace of Westminster in Wartime*
Unknown artist
Watercolour drawing, 1941 [WOA 2673]

Powerful search lights criss-cross the night sky above Westminster during the Second World War to identify enemy planes and defend this highly prized target.

© Saidman Illustrated

WARTIME REMINISCENCES

First-hand stories illustrate the strong personal connection many people have to Big Ben and the feelings the clock tower and its bells inspire. The following stories were collected to mark Big Ben's centenary in 1959 in a pamphlet published by the *London Evening Standard*.

Mistake that brought joy

During the war my fiancée and I had two meeting places, the clock at Victoria Station and Big Ben. We always used the meeting places alternately, and we always said on parting "See you under the clock". One afternoon I arrived at Victoria Station to find that a German plane had been shot down and had fallen right on the station a few yards from our meeting place. There were several casualties and the cannon shells from the plane were still exploding. I assumed all sorts of things happening to my girl friend and I searched all around the station for about an hour. Then somebody touched me. It was my girl. She had been waiting at Big Ben by mistake. I shall always have a soft spot for the old clock. James Simpson

Shock for the PC – and a bottle of Scotch as well

I was one of 50 Army officers, all amputation cases, occupying a first floor ward at St Thomas's Hospital, immediately opposite Big Ben in January, 1920. Our ward was to be disbanded [and] our problem now became urgent – amputees were strictly forbidden alcohol and we had to dispose of some 20 to 30 empty Scotch and other bottles with great secrecy. Operation Midnight Big Ben came into being under our trusty bombing officer. On the first boom of midnight six legless sportsmen each seized a bottle (grenade fashion) and with a good overarm action threw it smack into the dear old Thames. This was repeated twice. Then, alas, two bottles fell short and a very startled and annoyed policeman did not appreciate our disposal efforts. Dear old Major X threw a half a crown and whispered an apology and then wrapped up our last full half-bottle of Scotch in an old blanket and deftly heaved same into the outstretched hand of the PC. Big Ben completed his ponderous 12th stroke and all was well. Leonard W. Mason

My boy in khaki

I shall always remember Big Ben because it was under that clock in August, 1914, that I had my first meeting with the man I married. The first young soldiers of the war were marching along, whistling, singing and smiling. I looked at my boy friend, who was very smart in spats and buttonhole. Suddenly I realised that he might soon be wearing khaki and puttees and my heart missed a beat because he looked so gay and debonair that day. We married soon after and true enough, he was soon in khaki, and I was so sorry as it didn't suit him at all. He died young, but I shall always remember that meeting. Mrs G. Fuller

The last goodbye...

In December, 1915, I accompanied my soldier husband as far as Westminster on his return journey to overseas service. My husband looked up at Big Ben. That clock boomed as we stood there in sorrowful silence. In our last embrace, he said goodbye, never to meet again. K. Anderson

THE SILENT MINUTE

The Silent Minute was inaugurated on Armistice Day 1940, following a lobbying campaign spearheaded by Major Wellesley Tudor Pole (1884-1968). At 9pm, BBC radio broadcast the sound of Big Ben, which took about a minute to strike nine times. This was the Silent Minute – also known as the Dedicated Minute – a solemn period for reflection and prayer. In June 1941, a leaflet produced by the Silent Minute campaign said, *"The Big Ben silent minute provides men and women everywhere with an opportunity to unite in dedicating their every thought, word, and deed to the service of God and freedom."*

Bombing in the Second World War damaged the Belfry and blew the glass out of the south dial. Private Collection

The cover of a booklet which was printed to promote the Big Ben Minute. The cover was designed by Frank O. Salisbury. Private Collection

A view from the top

The buildings at the heart of the United Kingdom's constitution are laid out in this panoramic view from the Belfry facing west.

All three pillars of government – executive, legislature and judiciary – are represented, as are the church and monarchy which are historically the most important parts of the UK's constitution alongside parliament.

The Elizabeth Tower looks out over New Palace Yard, with its gates leading onto Parliament Square. The Supreme Court building is on the opposite side of Parliament Square.

Government, and other, buildings stretch away from Parliament Square to the right along Parliament Street and Whitehall. HM Treasury is on the corner of Parliament Square

and, further north, a corner of the Foreign and Commonwealth Office can be seen.

The centre of UNESCO's Westminster World Heritage Site is also captured. As well as the Palace of Westminster, the site incorporates Westminster Abbey, the Jewel Tower, which was part of the medieval Palace, and St Margaret's Church.

Westminster Abbey, with its two towers, is seen to the left. The Henry VII chapel with its Gothic decoration which inspired Barry and Pugin's designs for the Palace of Westminster's facades is the nearest part of the Abbey to the Houses of Parliament. St Margaret's Church nestles beside Westminster Abbey.

The roof of Buckingham Palace can just be seen to the right of the centre of the image above the trees of St James's Park.

The gilded decorative detail of the Elizabeth Tower in the foreground is an emblem of the royal Palace of Westminster, featuring a crown surmounted by an orb and cross. A corner of the roof of Portcullis House, the newest addition to the Parliamentary Estate, can be seen to the bottom right.

Deryc Sands for the House of Commons media and communications service

⌂ Cleaning the south dial seen from the Belfry above.

Heritage, Conservation and Maintenance

The London skyline includes many remarkable towers and spires but none more affectionately regarded than the Elizabeth Tower. This chapter explores the tower's distinctive architecture and design, as well as the work which goes on to preserve and maintain it.

ARCHITECTURE AND DESIGN

In his designs for the Houses of Parliament, the architect, Charles Barry, combined elements of classical planning, the Picturesque and the Gothic to produce one of the most famous buildings in the world. The whole Palace is part of the UNESCO Westminster World Heritage Site which also incorporates Westminster Abbey, the Jewel Tower, St Margaret's Church and Westminster School.

Barry's original design for the Palace included two towers, but no clock tower; royal palaces did not usually have such towers. Subsequent plans show that the design of the clock tower went through many changes: it was originally intended to house the Speaker's state dining room and decorative details were constantly revised.

London's skyline has changed dramatically over the past 1,000 years. In the 1860s, after the Palace of Westminster's two towers were completed, only St Paul's Cathedral was taller, making them the tallest secular structures in London at the time.

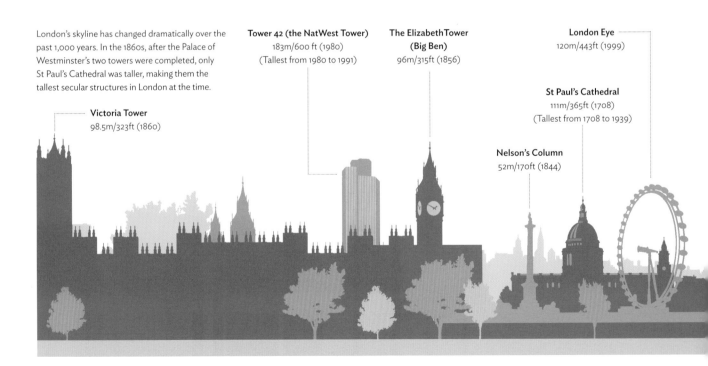

Tower 42 (the NatWest Tower)
183m/600 ft (1980)
(Tallest from 1980 to 1991)

The Elizabeth Tower (Big Ben)
96m/315ft (1856)

London Eye
120m/443ft (1999)

St Paul's Cathedral
111m/365ft (1708)
(Tallest from 1708 to 1939)

Victoria Tower
98.5m/323ft (1860)

Nelson's Column
52m/170ft (1844)

The tower stands 315ft (96m) high from its base at river level to the decorative finial at the top, and is about 40ft (12m) square. Its foundations rest on a bed of concrete more than 15ft (4.57m) deep, and the brickwork for the building begins 14ft (4.26m) below ground level to support the weight of the walls and roof, as well as the bells and clock machinery. The tower is constructed of brick and its walls are faced with Anston limestone from Yorkshire. Caen stone is used for the interior. The floors are supported by cast iron beams from the Regents Canal Ironworks in London. The sloping roof is made of cast and wrought iron. Its iron roof tiles are from the foundry of Jabez James of Lambeth.

The main parts of the tower's interior are concealed: two shafts surrounded by 20in (51cm) thick walls that rise through the building. A solid brick wall between them helps to strengthen the tower. The shaft on the north-west side of the tower is a disused air shaft originally designed to help to ventilate the Palace buildings. A brazier was kept burning at its base to draw used air through passages in the basement of the Palace and up the shaft to be expelled at the top.

The other shaft contains the pendulum pit and three weights. Sandbags at its base protect the floor in case the weights should fall. The pendulum pit (which is about 11ft long, 10ft deep and 3ft wide, or 2.4m by 3m by 1m) is suspended inside the top of the shaft. Clock mechanics can access the pit by ladder from the Clock Room. The base of the shaft is accessible through an arch leading into a chamber, which is the way Big Ben was brought into the tower. Today, the chamber contains two air compressors for the Palace's sewage ejector system which was installed in the late 19th century, and the tower is generally entered through a doorway to the south.

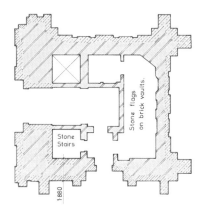

⌖ A structural plan of the ground floor of the tower shows the central weight shaft, stairwell in the south-west corner, air shaft in the north-west corner, and 'U' shape of the rooms curling around the central shaft on the eastern side of the tower.
Parliamentary Estates Directorate Archive

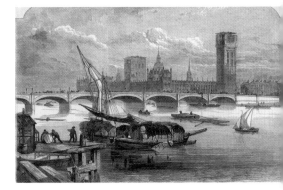

⌖ The towers were the last section of the Palace of Westminster to be completed. The clock tower took 13 years to build, It was a further seven years before the clock and bells worked together.
The Illustrated London News, 3 February 1855. Private Collection

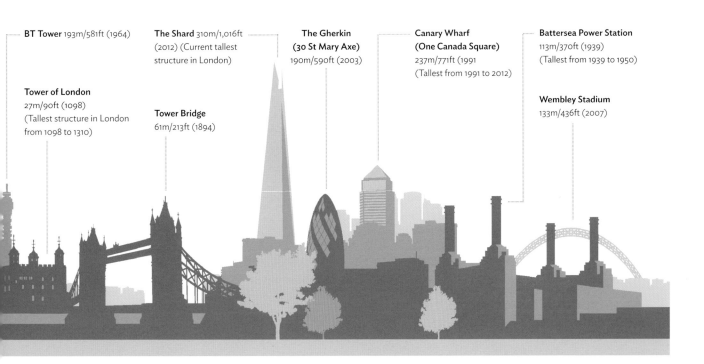

BT Tower 193m/581ft (1964)

The Shard 310m/1,016ft (2012) (Current tallest structure in London)

The Gherkin (30 St Mary Axe) 190m/590ft (2003)

Canary Wharf (One Canada Square) 237m/771ft (1991 (Tallest from 1991 to 2012)

Battersea Power Station 113m/370ft (1939) (Tallest from 1939 to 1950)

Tower of London 27m/90ft (1098) (Tallest structure in London from 1098 to 1310)

Tower Bridge 61m/213ft (1894)

Wembley Stadium 133m/436ft (2007)

The top levels of the tower – the dial surrounds, Belfry and the cast iron roof with its silhouette broken by the Ayrton Light's lantern-like room – are heavily decorated with painted stonework and gilded cast and wrought iron. Features include royal symbols and gargoyles.

DECORATION

As with the rest of the Palace, the tower's all-over decoration is a feature of the approach adopted by Barry and his collaborator, Pugin. Inspiration for the Gothic Revival design of the facades came from the ornate 16th century Henry VII Chapel in Westminster Abbey.

Narrow arches and slender columns rise between the windows up to the clock dials. Sceptres represent Parliament's authority. Ribbons of Gothic lettering form the French words *'Dieu et Mon Droit'* *('God and my right')*, the monarch's motto dating from medieval times, when Norman French was the language of the royal court. Unlike in the rest of the Palace, the Elizabeth Tower's horizontal bands of stone do not denote the position of the floors. The bands are decorated with Tudor symbols such as the portcullis, which appears throughout the Palace.

The clock level, containing the dials outside and the clock mechanism inside, projects beyond the wall below and is supported by brackets and a cornice decorated with ribbons and roses. The windows and recesses are deep, creating larger areas of shadow which give the clock dials even more prominence. Under each dial, a Latin prayer is carved into the stone: *'Domine Salvam fac Reginam nostram Victoriam primam'* *('O Lord, save our Queen Victoria the First')*. This was one of many decorative references in the new Palace to Victoria (1819-1901), who became Queen in 1837 and whose name came to define the era in which the Palace was built.

Above the clock level and Link Room is the Belfry with a tiny flying buttress at each corner. Seven arches on each side are open to the elements and unglazed dormers in the sloping faces of the roof above help the sound of the bells to ring out.

On each side of the tower, above the Belfry and the Ayrton Light, are eight shields decorated with symbols which represent the UK and its history: a thistle for Scotland, a shamrock for Ireland and a leek for Wales. The red and white Tudor rose representing England appears at each corner and the portcullis features beside the fleur de lis for France and the pomegranate for Henry VIII's first wife, Catherine of Aragon. The finial at the very top of the roof is decorated with foliage, an orb and a cross.

⊙ View south over the Palace of Westminster looking towards the central tower which was used for ventilation and, beyond it, the Victoria Tower which holds records of both Houses of Parliament dating from 1497.

⊙ Painted stone shields decorated with emblems feature above the Belfry and Ayrton Light. Botanical emblems include, from left to right: the rose for England; the thistle for Scotland; the shamrock for Ireland; and the leek for Wales.

THE CLOCK DIALS

The four cast iron and glass dials, each with a 23ft (7m) diameter, were one of the last elements to be installed. *The Times* reported in 1857 that each weighed 4 tons and was cast in six segments. The original pot opal glass – a type of glass with a milky white opaque finish – came from Germany, but was eventually replaced with glass made in Birmingham.

The minute spaces on the dials are each 1 ft (30cm) square and the hour figures are 2 ft (60cm) long. The hour figure of 4 o'clock is indicated by the Roman 'IV', probably at Pugin's insistence. This was unusual at the time: 'IIII' was generally preferred as it provided a closer symmetrical balance with 'VIII' (for 8 o'clock) on the opposite side of the dial.

The hands were originally made of cast iron, which proved too heavy so they were cast in bronze instead. The four minute hands were still too heavy so they were changed to hollow copper sheet. Each is 14ft (4.2m) long, weighs 224lb (100kg), and travels over 100 miles (160km) a year at its tip. The hour hands are made of bronze. They weigh 672lb (300kg) each and are 9ft (2.7m) long; as they are shorter, their weight does not affect their operation. The plain minute hands do not therefore match the ornate hour hands.

⤒ Each clock dial contains 312 pieces of pot opal glass.

↻ A clock mechanic carries out maintenance. Early electric lighting can be seen on the wall behind – c. 1910.

© TopFoto Picture Library

↰ The ornate 9ft (2.7m) hour hand dwarfs the men holding it. Scaffolding protrudes from the Belfry allowing the clock dial to be reached to remove the hand – c. 1900.

⤒ Detailing for the tower's decorative stonework is shown in this tracing of a finial and a window head – c. 1850.
Parliamentary Archives, BIR/3

LIGHTING THE DIALS

Until 1906, the dials were lit using 60 gas jets and keeping them lit was a dangerous and costly business. Gas burners manufactured by George Bray & Co. in Leeds were arranged over the walls in the narrow galleries behind the clock dials. They had to be lit by hand, which meant workmen climbing perilous metal rungs attached to the walls to reach them. One man was constantly on duty while the burners were operating to guard against fire. *The Times* reported in 1857 that the gas lighting cost £500 a year (equivalent to roughly £22,000 today).

Electricity was used to light the dials from 1906, six years before electric lights replaced the gas lighting in the Commons Chamber. From 1957, safer and more

⤴ Electricity was installed in different parts of the Palace at different times, but its first use in the building was an experiment in the clock tower. In 1873, a light was shone from the roof to illuminate the streets and to indicate when the House of Commons was sitting.
The Illustrated London News,
16 August 1873
Private Collection

⤵ A man cleans one of the 312 panes of glass in a clock dial. The photograph was taken in about 1900. The gas jets which lit the dials until 1906 may be seen to the left.
Curator's Office Archive

efficient cold cathode lighting was used. Today, each dial is illuminated by 28 low energy 85 W fluorescent bulbs with a life of 60,000 hours.

MAINTENANCE AND REPAIR

Time takes its toll, even on great timekeepers, and maintenance of the buildings is vital. The clock tower was first scaffolded in 1934 to repair damage caused by years of soot, smog and pigeons. The ironwork of the dials was cleaned and painted black, and the stonework surrounding them was painted and gilded. New pot opal glass was installed in the south clock dial in 1954 and, in 1956, the clock and Belfry received a much-needed overhaul after the buffeting inflicted during the Second World War. Corrosion of the bell frame and wear to the hammer assembly were also dealt with.

⊙ The tower was scaffolded in the mid-1950s for cleaning and repairs after being damaged in the Second World War. Part of the newly rebuilt Commons Chamber can be seen in the background. Curator's Office Archive

⊙ The clock hands have been removed in this early photograph of repairs to the dials.

Saved from a 160ft fall by just 2ft of rope

It was November, 1918. The war was over. Now the powers that be thought [Big Ben] ought to have a smarter appearance. My firm got the job to do the smartening up and I was detailed to get it under way. One of the first jobs was to get travelling cradles [to the outside of] each clock face so that they could be cleaned and painted. With my second-in-command I was going below one clock face when the rope ran through his hands and he lost control of his end of the cradle. When I looked at my end I found there was just two feet of rope between us and a fall of 160 feet.

J.W. Hallett from a collection of personal stories in a *London Evening Standard* booklet to mark Big Ben's centenary, 1959

From 1981, a programme of cleaning and repair of the exterior of the whole Palace was undertaken. The work on the tower began in 1983, was completed in 1985, and cost approximately £1.7 million.

To reach the top of the tower, 130,000ft (39,600m) of scaffolding was required, and repairs to the stonework required 105ft³ (3m³) of Clipsham stone from Rutland quarries. Some repairs were also needed to the ironwork. The regilding of decorated surfaces used 4,000 books of gold leaf, weighing a total of 4.5oz (128g).

The Historic Buildings and Monuments Commission advised on the decoration of the carving surrounding the clock dials, and the original red, green and gold designs were restored to the stonework. The Commission established that although the original colour of the metalwork forming the dials was blue, the two most recent colour schemes were black.

2007 MAJOR MAINTENANCE

The clockmakers discovered serious wear to the striking train and the escapement of the going train in 2006 while carrying out routine maintenance work and, in 2007, the most extensive repairs for 50 years were undertaken. For the first time ever, the clock would need to be stopped for several weeks to allow the necessary work to be done and the repairs were scheduled to take place before the clock's approaching 150th anniversary. Such a planned stoppage requires the clockmakers to secure not only the Keeper of the Clock's approval, but also that of both Houses of Parliament. The Speaker of the House of Commons and the Lord Speaker raised the issue in both Houses and permission was granted to stop the clock for seven weeks. During this period, the entire striking train and going train were dismantled. The parts which had to be repaired were then lowered down the centre of the spiral staircase. These included the worn barrel of the striking train and the escapement of the going train. The latter was completely rebuilt by the Palace clockmakers. None of the bells sounded during this period but a special electric drive unit was commissioned to keep the clock's hands going so that they told the correct time.

2009 BELL CONSERVATION

In 2009, Big Ben and the four quarter bells were conserved. The outer surfaces were cleaned using solvents and then given a coat of wax-based pigmented polish which was buffed to a shine. This protected the bells from the weather and from air-based pollutants and greatly improved their appearance. The conservators, as well having to climb up to the Belfry every day for five days, could work only in the short intervals between the chiming of the quarter bells and the striking of Big Ben.

The tower was scaffolded for cleaning and repairs in the 1980s. Parliamentary Estates Directorate Archive

The process of conserving Big Ben involved cleaning and polishing its surfaces. Curator's Office Archive

A conservator works on Big Ben in 2009. Curator's Office Archive

⊙ A historical analysis of paint samples taken from the dials and their stone surrounds in 1984 showed that the original colour scheme was royal blue. The dial surrounds were, however, repainted in black.
Parliamentary Estates Directorate Archive

COLOURS RECOMMENDED BY THE HISTORIC BUILDINGS AND MONUMENTS COMMISSION INSPECTORATE

RECONSTRUCTION OF THE ORIGINAL COLOUR SCHEME FOR THE CLOCK FACES BY THE INSPECTORATE OF THE H.B.M.C.
July 1984

⟳ The clock mechanism was entirely dismantled for major maintenance in 2007, exposing the whole of its cast iron frame. Private collection

⊙ The Elizabeth Tower as seen from New Palace Yard. The tower's tilt towards the north-west is too small to be clear to the naked eye.

↺ The hour hand on one of the dials is reinstated after repairs in the 1980s.
Parliamentary Estates Directorate Archive

The tilting tower

The Elizabeth Tower leans slightly from the vertical, although the building is perfectly stable. The tilt of 0.26 degrees was first noticed in 1965 when plans were made to build an underground car park for Parliament. At its top, the tower leans some 8 or 9 inches (20 to 22cm) from the vertical towards the north-west. A measurement was taken so that any shifting of the structure could be monitored.

Professor John Burland, a construction expert from Imperial College London who oversaw work on the car park said that the tilt *"would take 10,000 years to reach the inclination of the Leaning Tower of Pisa"*.

From 1995 to 1997, when the London Underground Jubilee Line was extended to Westminster, thousands of tonnes of concrete were used to prevent the work from causing the tower to lean more.

Parliament and the history of timekeeping

Parliament's role in the development of timekeeping reflects changes in the United Kingdom's broader interests. Timekeeping methods have existed since ancient times but, for most people, the passage of time was marked by the hours of daylight and the seasons until more disciplined approaches to timekeeping were required from the 17th century onwards.

THE LONGITUDE ACT

Britain's maritime trade interests expanded in the 17th century and finding a solution to the problem of longitude became pressing. Mariners could find their latitude – position north or south of the equator – using the sun and stars, but their inability to determine longitude – their position east or west – meant that many ships and their cargoes were lost.

🎧 John Harrison (1693-1776), a carpenter and clockmaker, invented the marine chronometer. It took him five years to build his first 'sea clock' (later called H1) which was trialled in 1736. Over the following decades, Harrison developed two further models, H2 and H3, then turned his attention to developing a more accurate and portable 'sea watch' *(see above)*. His masterpiece was sea clock Number 1 (H4), which is engraved with Harrison's signature and dated 1759. Captain Cook praised the copy of H4 which he used on his second and third voyages in the late 18th century.

Parliament passed the Longitude Act in 1714 to help find a solution. The Act offered a 'Longitude Prize' of £20,000 (comparable to nearly £3m today) which was never awarded, but several clockmakers benefited from other awards, in particular John Harrison (1693-1776). Harrison invented the marine chronometer in 1764 – a major breakthrough in the accuracy of timekeeping. The chronometer remained accurate to the time at a mariner's home port so that mariners could observe the sun to determine local time then compare it with the time on the chronometer to calculate longitude.

Initially, the technology required to make chronometers accurate also made them so expensive that few ships carried them, but by the mid-19th century, mass production by companies such as Dent's had made them affordable – Dent chronometer no. 633 accompanied Charles Darwin on board *HMS Beagle* in 1831.

🎧 *John Harrison*
Thomas King
Oil on canvas, 1767

La Reyne le veult.

[43 & 44 Vict.] *Statutes (Definition of Time) Act*, 1880. [Ch. **9**.]

CHAPTER 9.

An Act to remove doubts as to the meaning of Expressions A.D. 1880. relative to Time occurring in Acts of Parliament, deeds, and other legal instruments. [2ⁿᵈ *August* 1880.]

WHEREAS it is expedient to remove certain doubts as to whether expressions of time occurring in Acts of Parliament, deeds, and other legal instruments relate in England and Scotland to Greenwich time, and in Ireland to Dublin time, or to the mean astronomical time in each locality :

Be it therefore enacted by the Queen's most Excellent Majesty, by and with the advice and consent of the Lords Spiritual and Temporal, and Commons, in this present Parliament assembled, and by the authority of the same, as follows ; (that is to say,)

1. Whenever any expression of time occurs in any Act of Parliament, deed, or other legal instrument, the time referred shall, unless it is otherwise specifically stated, be held in the case of Great Britain to be Greenwich mean time, and in the case of Ireland, Dublin mean time. *Meaning of expressions relating to time.*

2. This Act may be cited as the Statutes (Definition of Time) Act, 1880. *Short title.*

Examined
H.C.M.
A.N.

William Rose

Cler. Par.

↻ Statutes (Definition of Time) Act, 43 & 44 Victoria I, c. 9, 1880 – the law which established Greenwich Mean Time as the official time across the whole of the UK.
Parliamentary Archives, HL/PO/PU/1/1880/43&44V1N94

↻ John Flamsteed (1646–1719) was appointed 'The King's Astronomical Observator' by King Charles II in 1675 and laid the foundation stone for the Royal Greenwich Observatory the following year. He catalogued over 3,000 stars and his observations led to the posthumous publication of a large catalogue, *Historia Coelestis Britannica*, as well as an atlas of stars, *Atlas Coelestis*. The post of Astronomer Royal still exists today. Unknown artist, Wikimedia Commons

↻ Parliament passed the Summer Time Act in 1916 to make the most of the hours of daylight by moving the time forward in the summer. Since then, clocks have been changed twice a year, moving forward by a hour in the spring and back again in the autumn
Parliamentary Archives, HL/PO/PU/1/1916/6&7G5c14

UNIFICATION OF TIME

The need to unify time grew with the start of the industrial revolution in the 18th century and the spread of the railway network in the following century.

At first, time was co-ordinated informally. The Royal Observatory started to transmit the time to destinations across the country using the electric telegraph in 1852, establishing the standard which became known as Greenwich Mean Time. The Great Western Railway applied a standard 'railway time' from 1840, using Greenwich Mean Time across its rail network and other railway companies followed suit.

By 1855, when the Great Clock at Westminster was completed, 98% of public clocks were set to Greenwich Mean Time. The new clock unofficially celebrated this informal standard.

Formal unification followed in 1880 when Parliament passed the Statutes (Definition of Time) Act. This established Greenwich Mean Time as the official time for the whole of the United Kingdom. GMT attained international status four years later, when the International Meridian Conference in Washington DC agreed on the Greenwich meridian as the prime meridian, making it the widely accepted centre of world time.

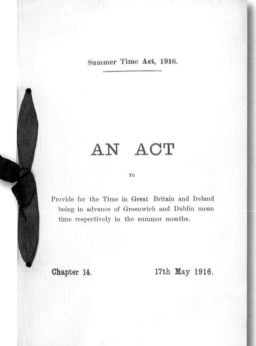

Summer Time Act, 1916.

AN ACT

TO

Provide for the Time in Great Britain and Ireland being in advance of Greenwich and Dublin mean time respectively in the summer months.

Chapter 14.   17th May 1916.

↻ The Longitude Act was passed by Parliament for *'providing a Public Reward for such Person or Persons as shall discover the Longitude at Sea'*. Commissioners were appointed with discretion to pay for experiments and award varying amounts to people who contributed towards discovering longitude. The reward for the first discovery was set between £10,000 and £20,000, depending on how successful the method was.
Parliamentary Archives, HL/PO/PU/1/1713/13An35.

Twenty nightwatchman's clocks were placed in the Palace's hallways until 1926. Nightwatchmen 'clocked in and out' by pressing the knob on top of the clock which pushed a peg in to mark the time.

'London's standard timekeeper'

In a letter to *The Times* on 8 January 1908, a correspondent complained about the inaccuracy of the *"lying clocks"* on public view in London. The following day, an editorial stated: *"So far as we are aware, there is no standard source of public time in London, and there is no time-ball dropped by public authority nearer than Greenwich. The great clock at Westminster is known to have an error, which is periodically corrected, of a very few seconds, and this is perhaps the nearest approach to a public standard timekeeper that we have in London."* On 17 January, *The Times* printed a reply from W.A. Pyall, the Secretary of Dent & Co., commenting that the great precision of the Great Clock at Westminster, which his company maintained, *"surely entitles it to be London's standard timekeeper."*

20th and 21st century developments

Today, atomic clocks are the most accurate known measure of the passage of time. They measure the frequencies electrons in atoms emit when they change energy levels. Coordinated Universal Time (UTC) has replaced GMT as the international time standard. It is based on International Atomic Time (TAI) calculated from some 400 atomic clocks kept by almost 70 timing centres worldwide.

PUBLIC ACCESS TO TIMEKEEPING

The changes brought by the industrial revolution meant there was an increasing need for accurate timekeeping. New technologies and production methods provided the means to meet this need.

Timekeeping devices became increasingly prevalent and, between 1750 and 1831, the proportion of the population owning one increased from 42% to 97%. From the late 18th century, as most types of work became mechanised, factories developed 'clocking-in' mechanisms so that workers began and finished at set times. Dent's company sold a type of portable 'tell-tale' or recording clock designed to ascertain *"whether a Watchman or other person whose duty it is to make periodical visits to different parts of an establishment performs his duty correctly"*.

The Royal Observatory introduced time signals in 1833: a ball dropped down a pole on the Royal Observatory building at 1pm every day for the benefit of anchored ships. Three years later, the Astronomer Royal gave his ward, John Henry Belville, the task of

sending an accurate chronometer around London to distribute the correct time to clock and watchmakers for a fee. Clockmakers could also visit the observatory to set the correct time on a pocket watch using the Royal Observatory's regulator clock – one of a number of extremely accurate clocks created by the best clockmakers to provide the best possible reference. Telegraph transmissions of the time from the Royal Observatory began in 1852.

Developments in the 20th century included the advent of broadcasting. The BBC introduced its 'pips' in 1924 – a sequence of six high-pitched tones sounded at one-second intervals, with the last, longer pip starting on the hour. A telephone service, the speaking clock – known as 'Tim' because the number dialled was 846 which, on old handsets, spelt 'TIM' – was introduced in 1936 and remains popular: it is rung over 30 million times a year and is accurate to one second in 3 million years as it is based on the time provided by the UK National Physical Laboratory (NPL). The NPL itself began 24-hour broadcasts of accurate UK civil time in 1950. Timekeeping has become an essential part of people's lives.

↻ The dial of a regulator clock completed by Vulliamy, Clockmaker to the Crown, for the Palace in 1823. The clock is a weight-driven, eight-day pendulum clock and the dial is typical of a fine regulator, having only the minute hand mounted in the centre so that the precise time can be read very easily. This type of clock and dials were often used in observatories, where reading the time accurately was important.

Notable clock towers

Clock towers around the world include some inspired by the one at the Palace of Westminster.

At 1,972 ft (601m), the tallest is the Abraj Al-Bait Towers, or the Royal Mecca Clock Tower which is next to the world's largest mosque and Islam's most sacred site, the Masjid al Haram in Saudi Arabia. Completed in 2012, its clock dials are the world's largest with a diameter of 151ft (46m) and minute hands which are 72ft (22m) long. The Harmony Clock Tower in Ganzhou, China, is said to be the world's largest pendulum clock and was commissioned from UK-based clockmakers Smith of Derby in 2009.

The Rajabai Tower in Mumbai, India was designed by the English architect Sir Gilbert Scott (1811-1878), whose grandson designed the House of Commons Chamber when it was rebuilt after being bombed in the Second World War. It was modelled on the clock tower at Westminster and completed in 1878. Several miniature imitations also followed construction of the clock tower at the Palace of Westminster. Amongst others, a cast iron clock tower resembling the Elizabeth Tower and known as 'Little Ben' (below) was installed outside Victoria Station in 1892. A silver replica of Little Ben was installed in Victoria, the capital of the Seychelles, in 1903 to mark Queen Victoria's Diamond Jubilee in 1897.

Photograph of Big Ben and the Houses of Parliament taken from the Victoria Tower by Benjamin Stone MP, June 1897. Parliamentary Archives, HC/LB/1/111/10/3.

This late Victorian photograph shows the tower above the roofs of the Palace; in the top left, a corner building has been decorated with awnings outside for the Diamond Jubilee of Queen Victoria.

The oldest part of the Palace, Westminster Hall, is pictured on the left of the image, the long peak of its roof running north to south. The large south-facing stained glass window of St Stephen's Porch is in the left foreground.

The surrounding area is recognizable today. On the right, Westminster Bridge leads towards Parliament Square. To the left, Parliament Street runs north from Parliament Square, with Government buildings on either side. It becomes Whitehall as it continues towards Trafalgar Square.

The Palace of Westminster remains outwardly largely unchanged since this photograph was taken in 1897, though significant internal improvements have been made to enable its 19th century buildings to accommodate a 21st century parliament and the Commons Chamber had to be rebuilt after bombing in the Second World War.

Pre-1000	1000	1200	1400	1600	1650	1700

Big Ben and the Elizabeth Tower

1367 – Second clock tower and first public chiming clock erected in Westminster

c.1707 – Clock tower demolis[hed] and 'Great Tor[...] bell taken to St Paul's

1099 – William Rufus completes Westminster Hall

1512 – Following a fire, the Palace ceases to be a royal residence

1292 – First clock tower erected in Westminster

William Rufus (1099)

Henry VIII (1491-1547, reigned 1509-47)

Edward the Confessor (c. 1003-66, reigned 1042-66)

Edward III (1312-77, reigned 1327-77)

Christopher Wren (1632-1723)

History of Timekeeping

c. 3500 BCE – Egyptian obelisks – early form of shadow clock or sundial

1685 – Revocation of the Edict of Nantes resulted in Protestant workmen moving to London

1764 – Joh[n] Harrison invents the marine chronomet[er]

Galileo Galilei (1564-1642)

c. 325 BCE – Greek water clock – the *'clepsydra'*

1094 – Su Song completes water-powered astronomical clock in China

1714 – *Longitude Act*

c. 3100 BCE – Stonehenge possibly used as a solar calandar

Christiaan Huygens (1629-93)

1675 – Royal Observatory at Greenwich established

1767 – Firs[t] *Nautical Almanac* produced [to] aid naviga[tion]

John Flamsteed, first Astronomer Royal (1646-79)

Related developments & inventions

c. 3150 BCE – Egyptian civilisation develops under first pharaoh

1642-49 English Civil War

1768-79 – Captain Coo[k] voyages to [the] Pacific islan[ds] Australia an[d] New Zealan[d]

1066 – Norman conquest of England by William I (the Conqueror)

1588 – Spanish Armada

c. 550 BCE – Athenian democracy develops

1492 – Christopher Columbus lands in America

960-1279 – China's Song Dynasty presides over advances in science and technology

1400s-1500s – Italian Renaissance

Isaac Newton (1642-1727)

c. **1440** – Gutenberg's printing press

Alexander the Great (356-323BCE)

1519 – Cortés arrives in Mexico

1685 – Edict of Nantes revoked

Marco Polo (1254-1324)

1800   1820   1830   1840   1850   1860   1870   1880

1834 – Fire destroys most of the Palace on 16 October

1852 – New Palace of Westminster opened by Queen Victoria

1854 – Clock mechanism completed

1885 – Ayrton Light installed

1836 – Charles Barry wins competition to design new Palace

1856 – Clock tower structure completed

1857 – First Big Ben cracks a year after being cast

1843 – Construction of clock tower begins

1858 – Big Ben recast and raised to the Belfry on 12 October

1846 – Competition initiated to build clock, won by Edward Dent in 1852

1859 31 May – Clock installed and officially started – hour strikes from 11 July and quarter bell chimes from 7 September – Big Ben cracks on 1 October

1863 – Big Ben resumes striking

1863 – Electromagnetic link to Royal Observatory

jamin Lewis Vulliamy (1780-1854)

dward Dent (1790-1853)

Charles Barry (1795-1860)

George Biddell Airy (1801-92)

Augustus Welby Pugin (1812-52)

Acton Smee Ayrton (1816–86)

Edmund Beckett Denison (1816-1905)

Queen Victoria (1819-1901, reigned 1837-1901)

1870 – Time zones created

1884 – International Meridian Conference adopts GMT

1852 – Royal Observatory begins telegraph transmissions of time signal

1833 – Royal Observatory introduces first time signal for mariners

1880 – *Statutes (Definition of Time) Act* – adoption of GMT as standard in the UK

1840 – Great Western Railway starts to apply standard 'railway time'

1840 – First electrical clock invented

1831-6 – *HMS Beagle's* second voyage with Charles Darwin on board

1859 – Publication of *The Origin of Species* by Charles Darwin

1876 – Alexander Graham Bell patents telephone

1851 1 May-15 October – Great Exhibition of the Works of Industry of all Nations held in Hyde Park, London

1750 – *c.* **1850** Industrial revolution

1837 – Charles Wheatstone and William Cooke invent an electric telegraph

1866 – First successful transatlantic telegraph cable

1844 First message in Morse code sent in the United States

1825 – First passenger railway opens between Stockton and Darlington

Edward VII (1841-1910, reigned 1901-10)

1900 1920 1940 1960 1980 2000 2020

Big Ben and the Elizabeth Tower

1906 – Clock dials lit by electricity

1940 10 November – Start of the 'silent minute'

1976 5 August – Clock mechanism fails: major damage caused to clock and chiming mechanism

2010 6 May – Live results from the general election projected on to the clock tower

1918 11 November – Bells ring at 11am to mark end of First World War

1945 Ayrton Light and clock dial lights relit at end of Second World War

2012 – Clock tower renamed the Elizabeth Tower

1919 11 November – Bells ring at 11am to commemorate Armistice Day

1959 31 May 1959 – Centenary

1892 – Little Ben, a miniature cast iron clock tower resembling Big Ben, installed outside Victoria station

1949 31 December – First television broadcast to mark New Year

2009 31 May – 150th anniversary

1941 Palace of Westminster hit during enemy air raid, destroying south dial – clock continues to operate

2004 20 March – Anti-war protesters hang banner beneath one of the clock dials

1913 – Electric winding motor installed

2007 –Restoration of striking and going trains

1923 31 December – Chimes first broadcast on radio to mark New Year

1910 20 May 1910 – First time Big Ben tolls for the funeral of a monarch – King Edward VII

1950 – Master clock system installed in the House of Commons

1995 – Energy saving lights installed with 28 bulbs per dial

History of Timekeeping

1902 19 March – UK National Physical Laboratory opens at Bushy House near London

1961 – Co-ordinated Universal Time (UTC) becomes the international time standard

1936 Speaking clock introduced

1890 – Central European Time (CET) begins – a time standard now used in most parts of the European Union

1955 – Louis Essen invents the first accurate caesium atomic clock

2001 – Demonstration of an optical clock, measuring frequency of a beam of light locked onto a single atom or ion, creates a new standard of accuracy in timekeeping

1960 – Time signals are coordinated internationally for the first time.

1924 – The 'pips' time signal first broadcast on BBC radio

1916 – *Summer Time Act* establishes British Summer Time

1950 – UK NPL begins broadcasting civil time on 60kHz frequency

Related developments & inventions

George VI (1895-1952, reigned 1936-52)

1957 – Sputnik I is first man-made object in orbit

2012 – HM Queen Elizabeth II's Diamond Jubilee

Winston Churchill (1874-1965, Prime Minister 1940-5, 1951-5)

Margaret Thatcher (1925-2013, Prime Minister 1979-90)

1914-18 – First World War

1939-45 – Second World War

1991 – Tim Berners-Lee makes world wide web available on the internet

1900 – First transmission of human voice by wireless

1925 – John Logie Baird transmits moving silhouette images

1994 – GPS becomes fully operational. Ivan Getting conceived the idea of a Global Positioning System using satellites in the 1950s

1927 – Philo Farnsworth makes the first working television system

1903 – Wright brothers fly first powered aircraft

1936 – First regular, public BBC transmissions begin from Alexandra Palace in north London

1897 – Queen Victoria's Diamond Jubilee

1962 10 July – Telstar 1 satellite launched to relay the first television pictures and telephone calls, and provide the first live transatlantic television feed.

Albert Einstein (1879-1955)